Do You Want to Know a Secret?

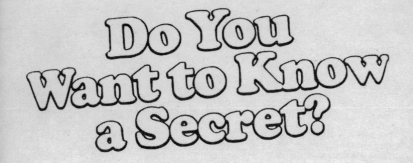

Do You Want to Know a Secret?

A Fab Anthology of Beatles Facts

Keith Topping

Do You Want to Know a Secret? is dedicated to Mick Lovell and Jeff Hart.

First published in Great Britain in 2005 by
Virgin Books Ltd
Thames Wharf Studios
Rainville Road
London
W6 9HA

A catalogue record for this book is available from the British Library.

Beatles photo courtesy of Corbis

ISBN 0 7535 1041 3

Typeset by Phoenix Photosetting, Chatham, Kent
Printed and bound in Great Britain by
CPI Mackays of Chatham, Kent

Contents

THE WORD
A Mod's Odyssey

Great music has existed ever since some caveman first banged two rocks together. It exists to this day and will continue to do so in the future, despite what some less-than-broad-minded critics may attempt to convince you.

However, that said, the Beatles (a popular beat-combo of the 1960s, you may have heard of them) were something different. Something special. Maybe a social phenomenon as much as a musical one, though that's the province of a different book.

The Beatles drew the limits for what a four-piece rock-and-roll band could achieve and wrote songs that will still be played after the great-grandchildren of everyone who first bought them are dead.

They also – to varying degrees – changed the world. Having done so, however, they then had the decency to split up and leave behind a legacy of some top tunes. As legacies go, it's genuinely not a bad one.

There are, literally, hundreds of books concerning every aspect of the Beatles' lives, career, recorded output and philosophies. They were an important band, so that's to be expected. Nevertheless, each new Beatles book must at least attempt to say something different about the subject, otherwise the author is doomed to repetition.[1]

Do You Want to Know a Secret? celebrates the fans'-eye view of the Beatles – a lot of love and respect for the product, close attention to detail, a healthy disrespect for a few sacred cows and a willingness not to take it all too seriously.

---

[1] I should make the point that – in common with many people who've written about them over the years – I've never actually met any of the Beatles. I did pass Paul in a corridor in Abbey Road and I once spotted George while he was shopping on Oxford Street. Words were not exchanged on either occasion. This isn't a book written by someone with inside knowledge of the Beatles as people. It's written by someone who was given 'Yellow Submarine' for his third birthday in October 1966 and never looked back.

Do You Want to Know a Secret?

So, at the risk of repeating what many others have previously stated, here are the basics:

The Beatles, like many of their contemporaries, began as a schoolboy covers band. If such a concept had existed in 1957 then the Quarry Men, featuring 17-year-old John Lennon, 15-year-old Paul McCartney and 14-year-old George Harrison, would have been an Elvis Presley/Chuck Berry/Little Richard/Johnny Burnette/Carl Perkins/Buddy Holly tribute group.

That they ever got out of Liverpool to a wider audience is a miracle in itself. That they did so by developing their own songwriting to replace the standards they played at the Cavern, around the dance halls of the Northwest and in Hamburg, is possibly the most remarkable thing of all.

Very few performers wrote their own material in the 50s – Holly and Berry did, but they were extraordinary exceptions. Songs were written by songwriters, who existed away from the day-to-day grind of performance and recording. If there's one aspect of the music industry the Beatles changed that is more significant than any other, it's probably this.

Lennon, McCartney and Harrison spent close to five years and numerous line-up changes honing their sound. They matured, thanks to a gruelling schedule and a determination to get to 'the toppermost of the poppermost'. And, let's not forget another important factor – they were, actually, *good*.

Gradually, the pieces fell into place; a manager who could get them a recording contract; a producer with a sympathetic musical knowledge who encouraged them to be adventurous; a succession of drummers up to, and including, Pete Best who, despite their efforts, all seemed to be occupying a seat that was destined to be filled by someone else.

In August 1962, Ringo Starr arrived. The rest is history. A hit. Another hit. Beatlemania. Conquering America. A film. Another film. MBEs. *Rubber Soul. Revolver. Sgt. Pepper's.* Brian Epstein's death. India. Yoko. *The White Album.* Dissolution.

If some enterprising scriptwriter had proposed such a story as a Hollywood screenplay the plot would probably have been dismissed as hackneyed – yet that's exactly what happened; they were, as Lennon subsequently noted, 'a band who got *very* big'.

Maybe we – fans and critics alike – think too much about the Beatles. Perhaps it's better that, for once, we ignore the social impact and the numerous, occasionally crass, attempts to shoehorn Lennon into some Gandhi-style role as the spokesman for his generation. (I believe it was Paul Weller who once noted that any generation in need of a spokesman isn't much of a generation in the first place.) Perhaps, we should also ignore the drugs, the infighting, the marriages, the Apple fiasco and the bitter court battles that followed. If the Beatles story teaches us anything it's that, ultimately, the only really important thing is the music.

In 1964, in the sleeve notes to *Beatles For Sale*, Derek Taylor pondered, in beautifully of-the-era sci-fi imagery, on the problems of explaining to someone from the future what the Beatles actually meant. 'Just play ... a few tracks from this album,' Taylor decided. '[They'll] probably understand what it was all about.'

That sounds about right. If, after reading this book, you want to dig out your scratchy old vinyl, or your shiny new CDs and remind yourself why you fell in love with this band in the first place, I won't argue with *that*. It's what I'll be doing.

Keith Topping
April 2005

THE LONG AND WINDING ROAD
A brief, but necessary, overview of the Beatles' place in pop history

Who were the lasting musical legends of the twentieth century? Joplin, Gershwin, Porter, Sinatra, Elvis, the Beatles ... After that it gets a bit arbitrary and difficult to find consensus. What *is* certain is that the Beatles, as a purely evolutionary force, led popular music into a new era.

They defined their own period not just with their music but by their very existence. As broadcaster Paul Gambaccini noted, the Beatles (with hindsight) could not have been part of the 70s, an era that, frequently, said 'no' to life. The Beatles, Gambaccini concluded, 'said "yeah, yeah, yeah".'

There are two distinct schools of thought on the Beatles' place in popular music history. One, articulated by several serious music critics, some dissenters and, on occasions, John Lennon, was that they were, indeed, just a band who got big. That they weren't especially talented musicians (no more than, say, the Searchers), but that they got by on their personalities, their haircuts and through being in the right place at the right time.

The counter-view is illustrated in the first edition of *The Guinness Book of British Hit Singles* (1977). Underneath the name 'Beatles', instead of the expected 'UK Male Vocal/Instrumental Group' the description reads: 'You *know* who they were.'

The Beatles were (and, forty years later, remain) famous. The only band in history of whom the vast majority of the people on the planet – even if they've never heard a Beatles record – will be able to tell you all of the band's individual names. 'How many Beatles does it take to change a light bulb?' George Harrison once asked rhetorically. 'Four. John, Paul, George and Ringo. That's the way it is.'

They're not, quite, the biggest-selling artists in history. But they are, probably, the most influential. It's impossible to imagine virtually any halfway important band formed since 1963 that doesn't owe its very existence – directly or indirectly – to the Beatles.

Without them, there would have been no Velvet Underground, no Led Zeppelin, no Sex Pistols, no Smiths, no Pet Shop Boys, no Oasis, no Westlife. There isn't a corner of the music industry, from record production and marketing to the concept of promotional videos and the creation of artists' own labels, that cannot be traced back to the Beatles doing it first.

They were trailblazers – sometime haphazardly, it must be said – but in the Beatles' story the tragedies are almost as spectacular as the triumphs.

Like all good stories, it had a beginning, a middle and an end.

The beginning was one summer's day in 1957.

A DAY IN THE LIFE
6 July 1957: How it all began

It's a hot, sticky Saturday afternoon. St Peter's parish church in Woolton, a relatively affluent district of Liverpool, is holding a garden fête. The entertainment includes the crowning of the Rose Queen and a display by the City of Liverpool police dogs.

Between these two events, at 4.15 p.m., a bunch of schoolboys appear on stage. They're a skiffle group called the Quarry Men (because most of them attend Quarry Bank grammar school). It's approximately their fourth performance and they are, frankly, not very good.

There's Colin Hanton on drums, Pete Shotton on washboard percussion, Len Garry on tea-chest bass, Rod Davis on banjo, Eric Griffiths on guitar and, standing at the front in a checked shirt, playing his Gallotone Champion ('guaranteed not to split') guitar, 16-year-old John Lennon. Who, by the look of him, has already had a few beers.

Remarkably, two separate documents of this apparently minor and insignificant event survive – a photograph (taken by Geoff Rhind) and a recording of two songs (Lonnie Donegan's 'Puttin' On The Style' and Elvis Presley's 'Baby, Let's Play House'), which Bob Molyneaux will keep for almost forty years before selling the tape to EMI for £78,000. Other songs in the Quarry Men's set include 'Come Go With Me', 'Be-Bop-A-Lula' and 'Maggie Mae'.

Somewhere in the crowd is a 15-year-old called Paul McCartney who has been invited by his classmate, Ivan Vaughan. Ivan is also a friend of the band and sometimes plays with them. McCartney is quite impressed with the singer, although it's obvious that he doesn't know the proper words to many of the songs he's singing and is, therefore, making up his own. McCartney thinks this is clever.

Later, while the band are waiting to do another set, Vaughan introduces his mutual friends. 'I was a fat schoolboy and as [Lennon] leaned on my shoulder, I realised he was drunk,' Paul remembered later.

McCartney, despite being left-handed, borrows someone's guitar, playing it upside down, and does his party pieces, Eddie Cochran's 'Twenty Flight Rock' and Little Richard's 'Long Tall Sally'. Lennon is particularly impressed that McCartney knows all the words.

A few days later Pete Shotton is cycling through Allerton and spots McCartney. 'John would like you to join,' Shotton tells him. McCartney asks for a day to think about it, then agrees.

The rest, for once, *is* history.

GET BACK TO WHERE YOU ONCE BELONGED
Some other essential dates

- 7 July 1940: Richard Starkey born at 9 Madryn Street.

- 9 October 1940: John Winston Lennon born at Oxford Street Maternity Hospital.

- 18 June 1942: James Paul McCartney born at Walton Hospital.

- 24 February 1943: George Harrison born at 12 Arnold Grove.

- 24 May 1957: The public debut of the Quarry Men, at an Empire Day party on Rose Street.

- 7 August 1957: The Quarry Men first play the Cavern, a jazz club in Mathew Street.

- 18 October 1957: Paul McCartney's first appearance with the Quarry Men (at the Conservative Club, New Clubmoor Hall).

- 13 March 1958: *Probably* George Harrison's first gig with the Quarry Men (at the Morgue Skiffle Club, Broadgreen).

- 9 November 1961: Brian Epstein, the manager of NEMS, a Liverpool record store, attends the Cavern (with his assistant, Alistair Taylor) and sees the Beatles for the first time. It would subsequently be reported that Epstein had been asked about the availability of 'My Bonnie' – a single the Beatles made in Germany with Tony Sheridan – by one Raymond Jones. For many years afterwards this story was believed to be apocryphal, although it now appears to be broadly true.

- 9 May 1962: While the Beatles are playing the Star Club, Hamburg, Brian Epstein meets George Martin, head of Parlophone Records, at Abbey Road. Sufficiently intrigued by the tape that Epstein plays him, Martin offers the Beatles a (provisional) record deal.

18 August 1962: Ringo Starr's first appearance after joining the Beatles (he *had* guested with the band on occasions previously when Pete Best was unavailable) at the Horticulture Society Dance, Hulme Hall, Birkenhead.

THERE'S A PLACE
Vital Beatles-related addresses

'Mendips', 251 Menlove Avenue, Liverpool

Aunt Mimi and Uncle George's home where John Lennon was raised, learned to play guitar and wrote many of his early songs. It was bought by Yoko Ono in 2001 and donated to the National Trust.

20 Forthlin Road, Liverpool

The home where Paul McCartney lived with his brother, Jim, and his father, Michael, from 1955 to 1964. Forthlin Street has a special place in the hearts of Beatles fans as it was in the front room that Paul and John wrote dozens of songs while playing hooky from school and college respectively. It was purchased by the National Trust in 1998. A shrine to a bygone era.

The Cavern, Mathew Street, Liverpool

Originally the cellar of a fruit warehouse, the Cavern opened as a jazz club in 1957. Under the subsequent ownership of Ray McFall, it began to feature rock groups and, by the time the Beatles played there for the final time (in August 1963), it had developed a worldwide reputation as the cradle of Merseybeat.

The club eventually fell on hard times and was demolished in 1973 to make way for a car park. By the 80s, however, with Liverpool attracting increasing numbers of Beatle-related tourists, it was decided to re-create the Cavern and it was rebuilt, more or less on the same spot as the original. It's now a thriving live venue (both Ringo and Paul have performed there in recent times).

Interestingly, directly opposite the Cavern was the site of Eric's, the nightclub where the next generation of Liverpool bands (Echo and the Bunnymen, the Teardrop Explodes, OMD, Frankie Goes to Hollywood, Wah!) got themselves together in the late 70s.

EMI Studios, Abbey Road, London

Hardly a day has gone by since 1969 on which four people (one barefooted) haven't attempted to re-enact the cover of *Abbey Road* while one of their mates stands on the nearby traffic island with his camera. Built in the 1830s, the building was converted into a recording studio by EMI a hundred years later. The Beatles recorded virtually their entire musical output there.

Twickenham Film Studios, London

The studio location for *A Hard Day's Night*, *Help!* and half of *Let it Be*. Twickenham was, additionally, the venue for many of the Beatles' promotional films. With director Joe McGrath, they filmed 'I Feel Fine', 'Ticket To Ride', 'Help!', 'We Can Work It Out' and 'Day Tripper' on 23 November 1965 for sale to television. Twickenham was also where the promos for 'Hey Jude' and 'Revolution' were shot, by Michael Lindsay-Hogg, in September 1968.

Kenwood, St George's Hill, Surrey

A 27-room mock-Tudor mansion on the outskirts of suburban Weybridge bought by John and Cynthia Lennon in July 1964. It became an essential part of Beatle-history via the many songs that John and Paul composed there.

7 Cavendish Avenue, St John's Wood, London

Paul McCartney's London residence from 1965 (prior to that, he'd been living with Jane Asher's family in Wimpole Street). Cavendish Avenue's close proximity to Abbey Road made it an ideal meeting place prior to sessions and a regular hang-out for the London 'In Crowd'.

'Kinfauns', Esher, Surrey

A luxury bungalow purchased by George Harrison in 1964 and the recording site of the (widely heard) *White Album* demos from May 1968. George and Patti were busted for cannabis possession in Kinfauns in March 1969 by the notorious Sergeant Norman Pilcher. Soon afterwards, George sold Kinfauns and moved to Friar Park in Henley, which was to remain his home until his death in 2001.

The Ad Lib, Leicester Place, London

The most well known of several swinging discotheques for the rich and infamous frequented by the Beatles and their friends in 60s London (others included the Scotch of St James, the Bag O'Nails and the Speakeasy).

The Ad Lib was a regular haunt for the pop fraternity as well as actors, boutique owners and the like, mainly due to a 'celebrity only' door policy and hardcore R&B music. The Ad Lib was the club that John, George and their wives went to after first being given LSD by George's dentist.

The Indica, Mason's Yard, London

An avant-garde art gallery and bookshop opened by John Dunbar, Barry Miles and Peter Asher in 1965. McCartney virtually lived there. Lennon got his copy of Timothy Leary's *The Psychedelic Experience* from the Indica and first met Yoko Ono in the gallery.

The Apple Boutique, 94 Baker Street, London

Opened on 4 December 1967, the boutique was to be, according to John, 'a psychedelic Woolworths' selling clothes, records, books and assorted hippie paraphernalia. The shop's elaborate external mural – designed by the Dutch art-collective The Fool (Simon Posthuma, Josje Leeger and Marijke Koger) – was deemed unsuitable by the City of Westminster Council.

A haven for shoplifters, it's estimated that Apple lost in the region of £200,000 before the Beatles closed it in July 1968. 'We came into shops through the tradesman's entrance, but we're leaving through the front door,' announced Paul.

34 Montagu Square, London

Bought by Ringo in 1964. Paul lived there for a while and subsequent tenants included visiting Americans like William Burroughs and Jimi Hendrix. John and Yoko stayed in the flat for some months in 1968 and it was there that they were busted for cannabis possession on 18 October.

Apple HQ, 3 Savile Row, London

A five-storey town house that once belonged to Lord Nelson (who used it as a love-pad with Lady Hamilton), the Beatles took up residence in June 1968 and made it the headquarters for Apple. If only *half* the things alleged to have happened within those walls over the next four years *did*, it would still have a remarkable tale to tell.

The Beatles built a studio in the basement (which, ultimately, caused the building to partially subside) and played their final public performance on its roof. Home to Derek Taylor's lavish media parties, John and Yoko's first publicity events and, for a fortnight around Christmas 1968, a gang of Californian Hell's Angels, Apple remains the Beatles last great folly.

WE ALL WANNA CHANGE THE WORLD
– The Beatles' LPs

Please Please Me (1963)

Legend has it that the Beatles debut LP was recorded in just twelve hours. Actually, that's not true. The bulk of the LP (ten songs) was, indeed, recorded in an all-day-and-a-bit-of-the-night session at Abbey Road on 11 February 1963 (along with an unused version of 'Hold Me Tight'). And, it is true that the throat-shredding 'Twist And Shout' was the last thing to be recorded and was captured on the first take.

However, the Beatles had already been into EMI on four previous occasions in 1962. The first, on 6 June, was merely an artists test ('Besame Mucho' from this appears on *Anthology 1*). A 4 September session produced the single of 'Love Me Do' and Mitch Murray's 'How Do You Do It?'

The version of 'Love Me Do' featured on *Please Please Me* together with 'PS I Love You' were recorded on 11 September, while 'Please Please Me' and 'Ask Me Why' were cut on 26 November. Additionally, George Martin's piano overdubs on 'Misery' and 'Baby It's You' were taped on 20 February 1963 while the Beatles were 200 miles away at a gig in Doncaster.

Please Please Me gives a reasonably accurate presentation of the Beatles' stage-act of the time. Although why two of their most popular live numbers, 'Keep Your Hands Off My Baby' and 'Some Other Guy' – both of which remained in their set well into 1963 – weren't recorded remains a mystery.

Bookended by two of the Beatles' most powerful rockers – 'I Saw Her Standing There' and 'Twist And Shout' – the LP showcases John and Paul's developing songwriting (the impressively mature 'There's A Place') and gives both George and Ringo a moment in the spotlight (on 'Do You Want To Know A Secret' and 'Boys' respectively). Raw and exciting, though with many obvious flaws (John had a cold on the day and, if you know what you're listening for, it's very conspicuous), *Please Please Me* is the sound of a band discovering the difference between studio and stage.

IS THERE ANYBODY GOING TO LISTEN TO MY STORY?
The Beatles' studio recordings pre-EMI

1958

The Quarry Men – Lennon, McCartney and Harrison, plus Colin Hanton and John Lowe (piano) – paid 17s 6d to record a two-sided 78rpm shellac acetate at Percy Phillips's home studio at 39 Kensington, Liverpool. They recorded Buddy Holly's 'That'll Be The Day' and the McCartney/Harrison composition 'In Spite Of All The Danger'.

The only copy of the disc remained with Lowe until it was purchased by McCartney in the 1980s. Remastered, if still somewhat scratchy, the two songs appear on *Anthology 1*.

1960

The Silver Beetles – Lennon, McCartney and Harrison, with Stuart Sutcliffe (bass) – recorded a number of rehearsals (mostly in March and April) on a Grundig tape recorder borrowed from a friend, Charles Hodgson, at Paul's home in Forthlin Road.

These performances – including rudimentary versions of 'One After 909' and 'I'll Follow The Sun' have featured on numerous bootlegs. Three songs – Ray Charles's 'Hallelujah, I Love Her So', Lennon and McCartney's Ink Spots-spoof 'You'll Be Mine' and McCartney's instrumental 'Cayenne' – appear on *Anthology 1*.

1961

In June, during their second residency in Hamburg, the Beatles – Lennon, McCartney, Harrison and Pete Best – were booked as a backing band for Tony Sheridan with Bert Kaempfert as producer.

Recording several songs with Sheridan over the course of two days, the Beatles were also given the opportunity to perform two numbers themselves; a beat arrangement of the 1920s standard 'Ain't She Sweet' and the Lennon/Harrison instrumental 'Cry For A Shadow'.

1962

On 1 January the Beatles had an audition with producer Mike Smith at Decca Studios in West Hampstead. Fifteen songs were recorded, including three Lennon/McCartney originals – 'Hello Little Girl', 'Like Dreamers Do' and 'Love Of The Loved'. The rest were made up of various examples of the band's eclectic tastes in cover versions.

IT WON'T BE LONG
The shortest recorded Beatles performances ...

- 0:22 'Her Majesty'
- 0:41 'Maggie Mae'
- 0:46 'Dig It'
- 0:52 'Wild Honey Pie'
- 1:05 'Mean Mr Mustard'
- 1:12 'Polythene Pam'
- 1:18 'Sgt. Pepper's Lonely Heart's Club Band (Reprise)'

LONG, LONG, LONG
... and the longest

- ⊙ 8:21 'Revolution 9'
- ⊙ 7:46 'I Want You (She's So Heavy)'
- ⊙ 7:09 'Hey Jude'
- ⊙ 6:28 'It's All Too Much'
- ⊙ 5:32 'A Day In The Life'
- ⊙ 5:05 'Within You Without You'

SOME ARE DEAD AND SOME ARE LIVING
Thirty important people in the Beatles' lives

Stuart Sutcliffe

John Lennon's best friend at art college, Stu was a talented abstract-expression-ist painter. John persuaded Stu to buy a bass and join his fledgling outfit. Possessing virtually no musical ability, Stu was still a vital part of the Beatles line-up circa 1960, creating the band's name and having a significant effect on their image (the fringe haircut, for example).

Having fallen in love with Astrid Kirchherr, Stu remained in Hamburg when most of the group were deported. There, he resumed his artistic studies. In April 1962, at the age of 21, Stu died from a brain haemorrhage. The Beatles subsequently paid tribute to his memory, including his photo on the cover of *Sgt. Pepper's*.

Bill Harry

Another of John's art-school friends, Bill was the first chronicler of the Beatles phenomena via his fortnightly paper *MerseyBeat*, which began publication in July 1961. Aside from giving space to John's writing talent, the paper was essential in helping to popularise and promote the Beatles locally. Bill has written several books on the band and remains a witty, informed source on their activities.

Pete Best

Born in India in 1941, Pete's family moved to Liverpool where his parents indulged Pete's passion for rock and roll by opening a youth club, the Casbah, in their basement. The Quarry Men played there regularly during 1959. Pete learned to play drums and, in August 1960, when the Beatles were contracted to play in Germany, he was hurriedly added to their ranks.

The evidence of his recording with the group suggests that Pete was a compe-tent, if not technically perfect, drummer and he certainly had a following among the group's early fans (particularly the girls).

He was fired, in controversial circumstances, in August 1962, just after the Beatles had signed to EMI and was replaced by Ringo. A variety of reasons have been given over the years but the simple fact was that Ringo was – ultimately – a better drummer.

Subsequently, Pete remained in the music business for some time, releasing several records in the US where anything Beatles-related was much sought after. The stigma of being 'the man who nearly made it', however, was always going to be a hard one to bear. In 1985 Pete (with Patrick Doncaster) published his memories, *Beatle! The Pete Best Story*, an amusing and observant warts-and-all account of his period with the band.

Neil Aspinall

A classmate of Paul's at the Liverpool Institute and, later, a friend of Pete Best, Neil was employed by the Beatles in December 1960 when they needed a roadie. Neil (and his van) were necessary to ferry the band and their equipment to gigs. 'You're one of us now,' he was reportedly told by John. Over forty years later, he still is. Their closest aide throughout the touring years, Neil became Apple's managing director in 1968, a post he holds to this day.

Astrid Kirchherr

A photography student and girlfriend of Stu Sutcliffe, Astrid's photos of the band in Hamburg capture the savage young Beatles in all their poverty-struck leather-and-jeans glory. Her half-in-shadow portraits of the band would, subsequently, be copied by Robert Freeman – at the Beatles insistence – for the cover of *With The Beatles*.

Astrid remained a close friend of the band, accompanying Paul, George and Ringo on holiday in 1963, being part of their inner circle during the making of *A Hard Day's Night* and spending time with them on their German tour in 1966. She also photographed George for the sleeve of his solo LP *Wonderwall*. Although for many years she lost control of the copyright to many of her most celebrated photos, Astrid's best work can now be seen in the book *When We Was Fab*.

Klaus Voormann

A graphic artist, Klaus first saw the Beatles at the Kaiserkeller and struck up an instant friendship with the band. Klaus subsequently learned bass and moved to the UK where his band (Paddy, Klaus and Gibson) was managed by Brian Epstein.

He eventually joined Manfred Mann and was an important part of the Beatles' entourage, designing the influential cover for *Revolver*. It was in Klaus's house that George wrote 'Within You Without You'. In 1970, there was much talk that Klaus would replace Paul in the Beatles. Although this never happened, he did play on many solo recordings by John, George and Ringo. Klaus also designed the cover-art for the *Anthology* project.

Jürgen Vollmer

Like Astrid and Klaus, Jürgen was one of the Exis, the Beatles' student following in Hamburg. He was a talented photographer, and most of the photos of the band in Germany that weren't taken by Astrid came from Vollmer's lens (the cover shot of John's *Rock 'n' Roll* LP, for instance). He moved to Paris in 1962 and it was there that a chance meeting with John and Paul led to them allowing Vollmer to cut their hair in a similar style to his own, thus inventing the 'Beatle haircut'.

Tony Sheridan

One of the first generation of British rockers, Norwich-born Sheridan was the guitarist in Vince Taylor's backing group the Playboys and featured on Jack Good's TV show *Oh Boy*. Relocating to Germany in 1960, he found himself sharing a residency at the Top Ten Club with the Beatles in April 1961.

Sheridan had been signed by producer Bert Kaempfert and, needing a backing band for some recording in June, hired the Beatles. Those half-dozen songs included a beat-arrangement of the traditional sea shanty 'My Bonnie Lies Over The Ocean'. Subsequent to the Beatles success, Polydor reissued the Sheridan recordings ad nauseam.

Bob Wooler

The DJ at the Cavern, Bob was a popular figure on Merseyside (it's his voice heard introducing the Big Three's 1963 *Live At The Cavern* EP). He would often supply the Beatles with records he thought they may be interested in covering. (He is, specifically, credited with introducing the band to Chan Romeo's 'The Hippy Hippy Shake' and Ritchie Barrett's 'Some Other Guy'.)

Wooler's association with the Beatles came to an abrupt end on 18 June 1963.

At Paul's 21st birthday party (held at the home of his Aunt Gin in Huyton), Bob and John Lennon had an ugly exchange concerning John's recent holiday with Brian Epstein in Spain.

According to Lennon, Wooler alluded to rumours suggesting that John and Brian were intimately involved. The violent altercation caused the Beatles some awkward publicity (the incident made the back page of the *Daily Mirror*). The matter was subsequently settled out of court with Wooler being paid £200 for his injuries.

Brian Epstein

With any other manager, the Beatles may never have got out of Liverpool. Brian Epstein was, as Lennon would later note, 'a theatrical, intuitive guy who presented us well'. Shy, Jewish and gay (at a time when homosexuality was still a crime in Britain), by the time he met the Beatles in 1961, Brian was successfully running his family's electrical goods and record shop (NEMS), but was still looking for a challenge. In the Beatles, he found his life's work.

There has been much speculation concerning Brian's motives in becoming their manager (did he fancy John?). However, what is certain is that once he got the position, he worked tirelessly for them and used his influence to knock the rough edges off the band, subtly changing their image (without, seemingly, changing their personalities) and getting them things they'd never dreamed of – radio and TV appearances, record contracts and US tours.

Signing the cream of Liverpool talent during 1962–63 (Gerry and the Pacemakers, Cilla Black) Epstein became an important figure in the London show-business scene. Although taken for a ride more than once by unscrupulous industry wide-boys, he was well respected for his charm and gentlemanly manner and, as has been noted, he helped to introduce the Beatles to film-makers, theatre people and establishment figures who would otherwise have been out of their sphere completely.

Marianne Faithfull has talked of how Epstein was seen as a big-brother figure (in the positive sense) by many involved in the beat-group movement. A wise and mature man surrounded by teenagers, able to advise and understand their problems. His tortured personal life was, for the most part, hidden not only from the public but also from the Beatles. But by the time that they stopped touring in 1966, Brian's role in their lives was gradually diminishing.

Nevertheless, his death in August 1967 (from an overdose of barbiturates that was almost certainly accidental) was a crushing blow to the Beatles – one from which they, arguably, never fully recovered.

Sir George Martin

If the term 'the fifth Beatle' applies to anyone, it has to be George Martin. Born in 1926, George joined EMI in the early 50s. A talented pianist, by the middle of the decade he was the head of A&R at Parlophone and made a reputation for the label with a series of comedy hits by artists like Charlie Drake, Peter Sellers and Bernard Cribbins. (It's often suggested that Parlophone was devoid of pop acts before the Beatles but that's a fallacy. The label boasted one of Britain's biggest solo stars of the early 60s in Adam Faith.)

A chance meeting with Brian Epstein in May 1962 – they were introduced by music publisher Sid Coleman – led to George signing the Beatles. He became their producer, musical arranger and interpreter of the increasingly experimental and unconventional ideas they presented him with.

As Peter Asher once noted: 'Sometimes George's genius was knowing when to jump in and offer musical advice; sometimes it was knowing when to go down to the canteen and have a cup of tea, letting them get on with whatever they were up to.'

Enough credit cannot be given to Martin; he spotted very early on the talent that he was working with. Besides his own instrumental contributions (think of any keyboards played on a Beatles record pre-1965, and chances are it was George playing), his innovative and clever arrangements for many songs were revolutionary.

George encouraged McCartney's interest in classical music and had his own imagination fired by the complex production ideas that Lennon would challenge him with (listen to 'Being For The Benefit Of Mr Kite' and you can, as John reportedly suggested, 'smell the sawdust'). An articulate and generous commentator on the extraordinary body of work he oversaw, Martin – who retired in 1998 – retains the affection of all Beatles fans. Without him, they would probably still have made it, but their records would have sounded very different.

Norman Smith

The Beatles' recording engineer from 1962 until *Rubber Soul*, Norman – along with George Martin – was responsible for helping to shape the sound of the early Beatles records.

He later became a producer, working with Pink Floyd on their extraordinary debut LP *The Piper At The Gates Of Dawn* in Abbey Road, while the Beatles were next door recording *Sgt. Pepper's*. In the early 70s, Norman reinvented himself as a singer, Hurricane Smith, and had a couple of huge hits in the UK.

Dick James

'He's another one of those people who thinks he made us,' John Lennon once said of Dick James. A pop star himself in the 1950s (he sang the theme song to the TV series *The Adventures of Robin Hood*), James became a music publisher and, via his friendship with George Martin, met Brian Epstein.

James set up Northern Songs to publish John and Paul's work. The deal would become the source of much bitterness between the songwriters and James. He sold Northern Songs in 1969 to Sir Lew Grade, something that John and Paul never forgave him for. To this day, the Beatles and their estates do not own the publishing rights to the vast majority of their own songs pre-1970. James subsequently formed Dick James Music and was Elton John's publisher. He died in 1986.

Tony Barrow

A Merseyside journalist who wrote a column for the *Liverpool Daily Echo* and was an early champion of the Beatles, Tony Barrow was hired by Brian Epstein as the band's press officer. Tony wrote most of the sleeve notes for the Beatles' early LPs and toured the world with the band trying, valiantly, to keep increasingly ridiculous press conferences under control.

Tony, who may well have been the person to coin the expression 'the Fab Four', also wrote the scripts for the Beatles' Christmas fan-club records and the *Magical Mystery Tour* booklet.

Mal Evans

A genial, Elvis-loving GPO engineer, Mal became a bouncer at the Cavern in 1962 ('he used to throw the Teddy Boys out', John would later remember) and struck up a friendship with the Beatles. When, in January 1963, the band had a radio session in London and Neil Aspinall was stricken with flu, Mal drove the Beatles to the capital.

On the way back, he impressed the Beatles when, in freezing conditions, the van's windscreen was shattered yet he still managed to get them home in one piece. Mal was promptly hired as Neil's deputy and became the Beatles' general gofer.

He accompanied them on tour and on holidays, appeared in *Help!* as the swimmer looking for the white cliffs of Dover, played the bass-drum on 'Yellow Submarine' and the anvil on 'Maxwell's Silver Hammer', may well have thought up the title *Sgt. Pepper's Lonely Hearts Club Band*, did production work for Apple (where he discovered Badfinger) and then moved to America. He died tragically in 1976 when he was shot by Los Angeles police after an apparent misunderstanding with his girlfriend.

Robert Freeman

A *Sunday Times* photographer who became John and Cynthia Lennon's neighbour when the couple first moved to Emperors Gate in London. Bob Freeman was, in effect, the Beatles' official photographer from late 1963–66. During that time he shot the innovative covers for *With The Beatles*, *A Hard Day's Night*, *Beatles For Sale*, *Help!* and *Rubber Soul*.

Bob toured the world with the Beatles in 1964 and his images of the band as they were on the point of elevation to iconic status are widely known.

Maureen Cleave

A journalist with the London *Evening Standard*, Maureen gave the Beatles some of their first national coverage, interviewing them in February 1963. Her relaxed style and admiration for the Beatles and their music impressed the band and she became a close friend and confidante, gaining intimate access to them during the next few years.

She was especially friendly with Lennon, who named her as his favourite contemporary writer in 1964. In March 1966 she published a lifestyle piece on Lennon, 'How Does A Beatle Live?' in the *Standard* in which John made his observation that the Beatles were 'more popular than Jesus'.

Geoff Emerick

Born in 1946, Geoff first worked with the Beatles as a 17-year-old tape operator. He became their recording engineer at the start of the *Revolver* sessions (devising the mixing of the tape-loops on 'Tomorrow Never Knows'), won a

Grammy for his contribution to *Sgt. Pepper's* and worked on *The Beatles* and *Abbey Road*. He also entered the production field with the Zombies.

Geoff became Apple's studio manager in 1970 and produced Badfinger for the company. He went on to work with Paul McCartney and Wings, America, Tim Hardin, and Elvis Costello and the Attractions.

Richard Lester

Born in Philadelphia, Dick Lester moved to the UK in the mid-50s to work as a director (and occasional actor) for the fledgling ITV network. Working on *A Show Called Fred* led to a lengthy creative partnership with Peter Sellers and Spike Milligan, including the Oscar-nominated short *The Running, Jumping, Standing Still Film*. In 1962 Dick, with producer Walter Shenson, made the musical *It's Trad, Dad*.

Chosen to direct *A Hard Day's Night*, Dick established a close working relationship with the Beatles. After *Help!* Lester went on to an impressive movie career, which included *The Knack and How to Get It*, *How I Won the War*, *The Bed-Sitting Room*, *The Three Musketeers* and *Royal Flash*.

Derek Taylor

Loved by Beatles fans as the humorous official mouthpiece for the band, Derek was a Liverpool journalist who became the show-business correspondent for the *Daily Express*. He ghost-wrote Brian Epstein's autobiography, *A Cellarful of Noise*, in 1964 and, for a while, became Brian's personal assistant and the Beatles' de facto press liaison.

He left in 1965 to work in America (his clients included the Byrds and the Beach Boys) before being persuaded back to the UK three years later to become Apple's publicity officer. Thereafter, Derek remained closely associated with the Beatles – particularly George – until his death in 1997. Derek co-wrote Harrison's autobiography *I, Me, Mine* and edited the *Anthology* book. His own – very entertaining – autobiography, *As Time Goes By*, was published in 1973.

Jane Asher

As a child actor, Jane made her first film, *Mandy*, at the age of five. Part of a theatrical family, she also played Alice in the BBC's 1958 *Alice in Wonderland*. She first met Paul McCartney in April 1963 and they began a relationship that lasted for five years. Paul lived for a while at Jane's parents' home in Wimpole Street.

Do You Want to Know a Secret?

Most of Paul's best songs of the era were inspired by, or directly concern, the ups and downs of his relationship with Jane ('And I Love Her', 'Here, There, And Everywhere', 'For No One', 'Things We Said Today', 'I'm Looking Through You' and 'We Can Work It Out'). Paul announced their engagement on Christmas Day 1967 and Jane accompanied him to India early the following year. But by July their relationship was over – Jane reportedly discovered Paul was having an affair with Francie Schwartz.

Jane's acting CV is hugely impressive – *The Masque of the Red Death*, *Alfie*, *Deep End*, *The Stone Tape*, *Brideshead Revisited* and *Runners* included. Towards the end of the 60s she established herself as a stage actress with the Bristol Old Vic. She also created her own range of cake-related baking products and wrote a couple of best-selling novels. She subsequently married artist Gerald Scarfe.

Barry Miles

Journalist and biographer, Miles first met the Beatles in 1965 at a birthday party for Allen Ginsberg. Barry was a partner, with Peter Asher and John Dunbar, in the Indica Gallery. Through Asher he became friendly with Paul McCartney, whom Miles would subsequently introduce to many of the key players in the London arts scene, including Robert Fraser, Richard Hamilton and Peter Blake.

With John Hopkins, Miles started the alternative newspaper the *International Times* in 1966. Miles was the label manager of Zapple. He wrote several books on the Beatles and in 1997 authored McCartney's official biography *Many Years from Now*.

Ken Scott

Like Geoff Emerick and Phil McDonald, Ken was just seventeen when he first worked with the Beatles – as tape operator on the *Hard Day's Night* sessions. He became their recording engineer on *The Beatles* and also worked on George Harrison's *All Things Must Pass* LP.

Ken's work as engineer and producer included recordings by Lindisfarne, Lou Reed, Elton John, Jeff Beck, Devo, Supertramp and, most famously, David Bowie.

Phil McDonald

Another member of the EMI production team, Phil was the Beatles' tape operator on *Help!*, *Revolver* and *Sgt. Pepper's*. He became their recording engineer on *Abbey Road*. Phil joined the exodus to work for Apple during the early 70s, and worked on many solo recordings by John, George and Ringo. He also worked as an engineer with Deep Purple and the Rolling Stones, and produced Squeeze.

Bob Whitaker

An Australian photographer who first met the Beatles in Melbourne in 1964. Invited to come to London by Brian Epstein, Whitaker took the cover photo for the US-only *Beatles 65* and the back-cover shot on *Revolver*.

As well as touring with the band during 1965–66 (he was at both Shea Stadium and the Budokan), Bob staged a series of surrealist photoshoots with the Beatles. One, taken at Whitaker's Chelsea studio in March 1966, produced the notorious 'Butcher' cover for the US *Yesterday … And Today* LP.

Yoko Ono

Japanese-born artist, writer and experimental film-maker. A product of New York's Dada-influenced *Fluxus* conceptual performance-art movement, Yoko's best-known works include her 1964 book *Grapefruit* and her 1966 *Film No. 4*. Often funny and always provocative, her work was highly regarded in the art world and she first came to the UK in 1966 to exhibit at the Indica Gallery. On 9 November, John Dunbar introduced her to Lennon.

The pair met at several 'happenings' during 1967 and, on 19 May 1968, Yoko was invited to Kenwood. The couple spent the whole night making sound-effects tapes (subsequently released as *Two Virgins*) and then consummated their relationship. They were married in Gibraltar in March 1969. Yoko is a tangible presence on many of John's late-period Beatles recordings. She even appears on a couple of them, including 'The Continuing Story Of Bungalow Bill', 'Birthday' and 'Revolution 9'.

Peter Brown

The best man at John's wedding, and mentioned in the lyrics of 'The Ballad Of John And Yoko', Peter was Brian Epstein's personal assistant at NEMS. Brown had the unenviable task of informing the Beatles of Epstein's death in 1967. He was later appointed Apple's Social Co-ordinator.

His 1983 book (*The Love You Make: An Insider's View of the Beatles*, with Stephen Gaines) was considered a betrayal by the surviving Beatles (Paul and Linda, reportedly, held a ceremonial burning of the book in their garden).

Linda Eastman

The daughter of a successful New York entertainment attorney, Linda became a photographer in the mid-60s, specialising in photos of British pop groups. She first came to London in 1967 at the invitation of the Animals and met Paul at the Bag O'Nails. A few days later she was one of the few photographers invited to the *Sgt. Pepper's* launch party at Brian Epstein's home in Chapel Street.

She and Paul crossed paths again in May 1968 in New York, and Linda moved to London in September to live with Paul at Cavendish Avenue. The couple were married in March 1969. Paul's partner, musical collaborator and muse throughout the next thirty years, Linda died from cancer in 1998.

Chris Thomas

Originally a musician, Chris became George Martin's assistant in 1968 and participated in the sessions for *The Beatles*. Although Thomas insists that he never actually 'produced' the Beatles, that's certainly how he's described on EMI documentation, particularly during a three-week period when Martin was on holiday in September 1968.

Chris also played harpsichord on 'Piggies', keyboards on 'Savoy Truffle' and 'Long Long Long' and Mellatron on 'The Continuing Story Of Bungalow Bill'. He became a much sought-after producer, working with Roxy Music, the Sex Pistols, the Pretenders, Elton John and Pulp. He also worked with McCartney on 1979's *Back To The Egg*.

Phil Spector

Arguably pop music's most renowned producer, Spector had his first hit at eighteen – the Teddy Bears' 'To Know Him Is To Love Him'. His subsequent career with the Ronettes, the Crystals, the Righteous Brothers and Ike and Tina Turner introduced his 'wall of sound' productions to the public.

He first worked with John Lennon on the 1970 Plastic Ono Band single 'Instant Karma'. Lennon then asked Spector to salvage the *Let It Be* tapes, which Spector did – with what can most charitably be described as mixed results. He spent most of the early 70s working on solo recordings by Lennon and Harrison.

In 2003 Spector was arrested in connection with the death of actress Lana Clarkson and is, at the time of writing, awaiting trial.

WE ALL WANNA CHANGE THE WORLD
– The Beatles' LPs

With The Beatles (1963)

Recorded on odd days between concerts up and down the country from 18 July to 23 October 1963. The piecemeal nature of the *With The Beatles* sessions makes it even more remarkable that the finished LP – with its hugely influential cover – has such a polished feel. George Martin has described it as 'the first songbook', a showcase for the band's diversity and talent. It's certainly that.

The fourteen songs (the sessions also produced the 'I Want To Hold Your Hand'/'This Boy' single) give a strong flavour of the Beatles eclectic tastes. Three of the covers are from Berry Gordy's Tamla-Motown stable, the Beatles being among the first white acts to acknowledge its existence. Lennon's interpretation of Smokey Robinson's 'You've Really Got A Hold On Me' is one of the LP's highlights.

While there were the expected conceits (every beat group in the country covered 'Roll Over Beethoven'), the inclusion of a Broadway standard like 'Till There Was You' was a clever piece of opportunism, showcasing a different side of the Beatles to an entirely new audience.

It's with the self-penned material, though, that *With The Beatles* really shines. 'All My Loving', 'It Won't Be Long' and 'Not A Second Time' were the kind of songs that other bands would have given their right arm to have as singles. George's first composition, the obstinate 'Don't Bother Me', is another unexpected treat.

With The Beatles was a giant step forward from both the sound and the vision of *Please Please Me*. Essential listening.

WHILE MY GUITAR GENTLY WEEPS
Who played what

In the early days it was all so simple. Ringo played his Ludwig drums, Paul his left-handed Hofner bass, John his Rickenbacker guitar and any harmonica that was required, and George the lead guitar (usually a Gretsch, sometimes a Rickenbacker 12-string, occasionally a Gibson semi-acoustic for the slower songs). If the Beatles needed any piano on their records, George Martin played it. That's the way the situation stayed throughout 1963 and most of 1964.

The possibilities offered by multitrack studio recording, however, changed all that (even if the band were still only using four-track until 1968). This was particularly useful to McCartney – a decent pianist and guitarist and a more than passable drummer. Lennon, too, soon learned his way around a keyboard.

Paul, as a guitarist, can be heard on many Beatles songs, including 'Ticket To Ride', 'Drive My Car', 'Taxman', 'Sgt. Pepper's Lonely Hearts Club Band', 'Fixing A Hole' and 'The End'. He usually played an Epiphone Casino – which he acquired, at the suggestion of John Mayall, around Christmas 1964 – and, later, a Fender Esquire.

George first tinkered with a sitar on the set of *Help!* He was introduced to the work of sitar virtuoso Ravi Shankar by his friend Dave Crosby of the Byrds in August 1965. Harrison was so taken with the instrument's exotic sound that, on returning to London, he bought a cheap sitar at a shop called India Craft on Oxford Street and worked out how to play it.

It was first used – memorably – on 'Norwegian Wood' and then on George's own ragas 'Love You To' and 'Within You Without You'. George played another Indian instrument, the tambura (a four-stringed lute which produces a distinctive tonic drone), on 'Tomorrow Never Knows', while he tried his hand at violin on 'All You Need Is Love'.

Ringo's lack of mastery of the Hammond organ can be heard on 'I'm Looking Through You', while George played Hammond on several numbers, including 'It's All Too Much', 'Blue Jay Way', 'While My Guitar Gently Weeps' and 'Old Brown Shoe'.

One of the most admired instrumental passages on a Beatles record was Paul's Mellatron opening to 'Strawberry Fields Forever'. Always a keen drummer, Paul can be heard tub-thumbing on 'Back In The USSR', 'Dear Prudence', 'Martha My Dear' and 'The Ballad Of John And Yoko' among others.

With Paul often playing keyboards on late-period Beatles songs, sometimes John or George would be called upon to fill in on bass. Right-handed Burns Nu-Sonic and Fender VI basses were acquired for such eventualities. Thereafter, John played bass on 'Rocky Raccoon', 'Back In The USSR', 'Let It Be' and 'The Long And Winding Road'. George handled the instrument on 'She Said She Said', 'Hey Jude', 'Birthday', 'Honey Pie' and 'Golden Slumbers'.

TELL ME WHAT YOU SEE
Famous Beatles gigs

18 August – 27 November 1960, the Indra Club/ Kaiserkeller, Hamburg

Arriving in Hamburg as an inexperienced combo, the Beatles settled into a two-month residency at Bruno Koschmider's Indra (a fleapit with a reputation lower than rattlesnake's piss). Thereafter, they played two further months at the only slightly more salubrious Kaiserkeller until – in the wake of George, Paul and Pete getting deported – they returned to Liverpool.

It must have been a hell of a sight; five young lads fresh off the boat playing up to seven hours a night of furious rock and roll in the surroundings of the Reeperbahn. 'Hamburg was like Blackpool,' noted Paul. 'Except with strip clubs!'

Developing an audience composed largely of drunken sailors, flick-knife-wielding gangsters, prostitutes and (quite unexpectedly) a bunch of art students called Exis, the Beatles expanded their set to include show tunes, jazz and blues songs; anything, in fact, to entertain people.

At the Kaiserkeller they shared the bill with Rory Storm and the Hurricanes – featuring Ringo Starr on drums – and a competition began as to who could demolish the wooden stage first. Rory won, much to Lennon's chagrin.

Encouraged by Koschmider to '*Mach schau!*' and fuelled by a surfeit of alcohol and slimming pills (Preludin) that they'd been given to help them stay awake, the Beatles become a noisy, energetic proto-punk band. By the time they returned home, they were *red hot*.

27 December 1960, Litherland Town Hall

'Direct from Hamburg', said the posters, and most of the crowd assumed the Beatles were, in fact, German, commending the band on their excellent English. Booked by Bob Wooler and Brian Kelly, this was the night that the Beatles legend was born.

The band (still a five-piece, including temporary bassist Chas Newby) played an electrifying set to an enthusiastic crowd that included many people who would subsequently form Merseybeat bands after being inspired by the Beatles.

As with the Pistols at the 100 Club, if everyone who now claims to have attended *had* actually been there, Litherland Town Hall would have had an audience on the scale of Woodstock.

9 February 1961, The Cavern

The Beatles' first appearance at the venue with which they would become most associated was somewhat low key, a lunchtime session that wasn't even advertised. The band would play the Cavern around 300 times.

1 April – 30 June 1961, Top Ten Club, Hamburg

Their second Hamburg residency was at the much smarter Top Ten, run by Peter Eckhorn, although the Beatles took most of their loyal fan base with them from the Kaiserkeller. It was during this period that Paul acquired his Hofner bass and John his Rickenbacker and, via Astrid Kirchherr's influence on Stu, the band began to experiment with the Gene Vincent-style black-leather look.

Again, the Hurricanes and Ringo were around, as was Tony Sheridan with whom the Beatles often jammed. This eventually led to their first professional recording session.

22 August 1962, The Cavern

The day that Granada TV cameras captured a moment of history. This was Ringo's fourth gig with the Beatles and, as an incendiary version of 'Some Other Guy' ends, someone in the audience shouts 'We want Pete!' George was, reportedly, butted in the face by one outraged fan and publicity photographs taken around this time show him sporting a magnificent black eye.

28 October 1962, Liverpool Empire

The Beatles first theatre-sized show before a home-town crowd. Ostensibly, they were supporting visiting superstar Little Richard, but everyone knew who the *real* headliners were.

18 April 1963, Royal Albert Hall

The Beatles topped the bill at a BBC radio concert (*Swinging Sound '63*). It was an important date for a number of reasons. Firstly, one of the other acts was

American singer Del Shannon, who was so impressed by what he heard that he went back to the States and recorded a cover of 'From Me To You'. Also, the *Radio Times* sent along the 17-year-old actress Jane Asher to write a piece about the Beatles – within days she and McCartney were an item.

Finally, the Beatles had met the Rolling Stones four days earlier at the Crawdaddy Club and had given them tickets to this event. By way of thanks, Brian Jones gave Neil and Mal a hand with the instruments after the show and was mistaken for a Beatle by several girls, who promptly mobbed him. From that moment onwards Brian, reportedly, wanted to do nothing other than be a pop star.

4 November 1963, Royal Variety Performance

The most bloatedly 'showbiz' event possible (other guests included Joe Loss and Max Bygraves) was turned, via some cheeky-monkey comments, into the Beatles' elevation to establishment heroes.

McCartney couldn't keep his head still through 'Till There Was You' (though he made up for it with a cruel – albeit funny – joke about Sophie Tucker, 'our favourite American group'). But the clincher was Lennon, introducing 'Twist And Shout' with instructions to the royal box to 'rattle your jewellery'. The Queen Mum loved them so, from now on, everyone else had to. It was The Law.

20 November 1963, ABC Cinema, Manchester

There's no finer capturing of the flowering of Beatlemania in Britain than the few moments of this show, filmed as part of a Pathé News feature, *The Beatles Come To Town*. Frothing-at-the-mouth versions of 'She Loves You' and 'Twist And Shout' were accompanied by a plethora of shots of hysterical girls, all in glorious Technicolor. The Beatles never looked prettier, the noise they made never sounded more knicker-wettingly fabulous.

17 January – 4 February 1964, Olympia Theatre, Paris

'We expected French girls – oo-la-la,' noted George. 'Instead, hanging around the stage door were lots of slightly gay-looking boys shouting "Ringo!"' The two-week Paris residency – on a bill with Sylvie Vartan and Trini Lopez – was eventually considered a success (although the French papers gave the Beatles a hard time for the first few days).

11 February 1964, Washington Coliseum

The Beatles' first American concert – filmed by CBS and shown in cinemas across the US a month later. Because the stage was situated in the middle of the hall to allow more people in, the Beatles had to keep repositioning themselves (and Ringo's drums) every few songs.

17 June 1964, Festival Hall, Melbourne

With Ringo having just rejoined the band after his tonsil-related lay-off, this extraordinary show was filmed for Australian TV (*The Beatles Sing for Shell*). It's a terrific performance – check out the version of 'You Can't Do That' on *Anthology*. There's a particularly funny moment when a besuited Aussie runs on stage during 'Long Tall Sally' and shakes John's hand.

16 August 1964, Blackpool Opera House

What a gig *this* must have been. The support acts were the High Numbers (soon to become the Who) and the Kinks. As if that wasn't enough, the kids of Blackpool got the Beatles as well.

23 August 1964, Hollywood Bowl

Recorded by Capitol and, many years later, partially released on LP (*The Beatles At The Hollywood Bowl*). The sound of 18,700 screaming girls marginally failed to drown out the Beatles' fabulous noise. Some amateur film footage of the show also exists. There was a near riot after the show and further trouble on Sunset Boulevard with the LAPD imposing a 10 p.m. curfew.

24 December 1964 – 16 January 1965, Hammersmith Odeon

A fortnight's residency for *Another Beatles Christmas Show*. The compere was Jimmy Saville and other acts included a teenage Elkie Brooks, Freddie and the Dreamers and the Yardbirds (it was during these shows that Harrison and Eric Clapton began a friendship that would last for the rest of George's life).

11 April 1965, Empire Pool, Wembley

The annual *New Musical Express* Poll-Winners show (filmed by ABC and broadcast a week later). The Beatles looked fantastic in their beige high-collared jackets, powering through 'I Feel Fine', 'She's A Woman', 'Baby's In Black', 'Ticket To

Ride' and 'Long Tall Sally'. They were also presented with their Best Group award by Tony Bennett.

15 August 1965, Shea Stadium, New York

Immortalised on celluloid – *The Beatles at Shea Stadium* – there is no more perfect advert for the scale and lunacy of Beatlemania at its most American. The Beatles are actually quite tuneful considering the cacophony they're in the midst of. But it's the spectacle of the venue – and the 55,600 crowd – that hammer home how *big* Shea Stadium was.

The best moment is the encore, 'I'm Down': John playing the organ with his elbow à la Jerry Lee Lewis and George, helpless with laughter. Three minutes of pure indulgence from four young men who simultaneously realised that, at this moment in history, they were simply *the business*.

A video of this show should be given to anyone who's ever wanted to be a pop star. Remember, a guitar's all right for a hobby but you'll never make a living at it.

29 August 1966, Candlestick Park, San Francisco

The final date on the hideous last American tour before an audience of 25,000. In the same month that *Revolver* was released, the Beatles were still opening their shows with 'Rock And Roll Music' and closing with 'Long Tall Sally', covers which had been the staple of their live act seven years earlier in the Cavern.

They knew this was to be their last live performance for a long time (if not ever). Both John and Paul took cameras on stage with them and they asked Tony Barrow to record the concert on his portable cassette.

29 January 1969, Savile Row

Needing a climax to the *Let It Be* movie, after dozens of potential sites for a one-off concert had been rejected, Paul, John and Ringo persuaded George to come up onto the roof of Apple (on one of the coldest days in living memory) and play live one final time. Of course, nobody had bothered to inform the police and they turned up thirty minutes later to ask if the band wouldn't mind awfully turning the noise down.

Before that, together with Billy Preston, the Beatles produced serviceable recordings of 'I've Got A Feeling', 'One After 909', 'Dig A Pony', a hilarious ad-libbed version of 'Get Back' and some visual images that are still regularly ripped off by bands to this day.

SEE HOW THEY RUN
... and some infamous ones

20 May 1960, Town Hall, Alloa

Having attended an audition for London impresario Larry Parnes on 10 May, the Silver Beetles (John, Paul, George, Stu Sutcliffe and drummer Tommy Moore) were hired for a two-week tour of Scotland backing one of Parnes's singers, Johnny Gentle. Paul, George and Stu promptly changed their names, perhaps expecting instant stardom.

Sadly, the tour was a disaster of small audiences, poor performances and a traffic accident that left Moore concussed – he had to be, literally, dragged from a hospital bed to play at Aberdeen on 23 May. 'We were crummy,' George subsequently noted. 'We were like orphans, our shoes were full of holes!'

30 May 1960, Jacaranda Coffee Bar, Liverpool

The Silver Beetles were booked by Allan Williams when his resident combo, the Royal Caribbean Steel Band, were otherwise engaged. Legend has it their 'payment' was a can of Coca-Cola and a plate of beans on toast. Each.

11 June 1960, The Grosvenor, Lisgard

With the group temporarily drummerless – after Moore decided his future lay in a job at Garston Bottle Works – this gig turned into farce when John asked the audience if anyone could play drums.

One local tough, a notorious character called Ronnie, decided he would have a go and proceeded to bash incompetently away for a while until Allan Williams plucked up the courage to ask him to leave.

July 1960, Upper Parliament Street, Liverpool

The exact date of this performance is unknown. Williams and his partner, Lord Woodbine, ran an illegal strip club and the Silver Beetles were offered ten shillings a night each to provide backing music for a stripper called Janice. Given sheet music (which none of them could read) the band — with Paul on drums — played instrumentals like 'The *Third Man* Theme', 'Moonglow' and 'Ramrod'.

9 December 1961, Aldershot

The Beatles' first UK show outside the Merseyside area was a complete disaster when the local paper declined to run an advert. In the event, the Beatles played to a reported audience of eighteen.

2 December 1962, Embassy Cinema, Peterborough

Even with a record in the charts, booking the Beatles as a support act to Australian yodeller Frank Ifield and on the same package-bill as the Tommy Wallis and Beryl Xylophone Team probably wasn't the best idea Brian Epstein ever had.

The Beatles certainly failed to excite local journalist Lyndon Whittaker, who wrote that 'the drummer … made far too much noise'.

2 December 1963, Grosvenor Hotel, London

Another example of Epstein trying out the Beatles in an alien environment; in this case a charity cabaret floor show at this plush hotel in Park Lane. Surrounded by a bored-looking audience in evening dress, the Beatles rushed through a seven-song set and, reportedly, asked Brian never to book them on this type of show again.

1 July 1966, The Budokan, Tokyo

Having hardly played live since the autumn of the previous year, the 1966 world tour was a shattering blow to the Beatles' collective ego. They just about got away with the German leg, their lack of instrumental practice covered by the screams, but when they got to Japan where the audience (on pain of instant ejection) were quieter, all the band's mistakes were cruelly exposed.

This concert, filmed by Japanese television, is genuinely painful to watch. Great songs being ritually murdered by poor amplification, clumsy playing and downright incompetent singing (you can't *do* that to 'If I Needed Someone' — it's *wrong*).

4 July 1966, Rizel Football Stadium, Manila

And it got worse. A two-day trip to Ferdinand Marcos's military dictatorship in the Philippines turned into a nightmare when the band decided not to attend an official function at the Malacanang Palace with the President's shoe-loving wife, Imelda.

Though the gig itself (in front of 50,000 people) passed off relatively uneventfully, the next day at the airport, the Beatles and their entourage were manhandled (driver Alf Bicknell got kicked in the ribs). John and Ringo reportedly cowered behind some nuns for safety.

Even when the Beatles got on the plane, Brian Epstein, Mal Evans and Tony Barrow were held behind to pay a huge 'leaving the country' tax. Full of pent-up loathing when they arrived back at Heathrow, George Harrison's memorable reply to a question about what they would be doing next was, 'We're gonna have a couple of weeks to recuperate before we go and get beaten up by the Americans.'

19 August 1966, Mid-South Coliseum, Memphis, Tennessee

You shouldn't joke about those things. The American tour began with Beatles records being burned in the south in reaction to John's 'Jesus' quote. A somewhat bemused apology at Chicago airport and the fact that most of the early part of the tour was taking place in the northern states helped to calm the situation.

But when the Beatles finally ventured south, it was open season for the nutters. Outside this show, robed Ku Klux Klansmen were proclaiming that, as a terror organisation, they intended to stop the event, while a preacher, the Reverend Stroad, held a rally to protest at 'the blasphemous Beatles'.

Inside, things reached an apocalyptic climax when a firecracker landed near the stage and exploded. For one awful second the Beatles all looked at each other wondering which of them had been shot.

YER BLUES
John Lennon – middle-class hero

It's probably best to get this out of the way at the beginning. John Lennon was – by his own admission – at various times, an alcoholic, a beater of women and a heroin addict. He was also a man who devoted a sizeable proportion of his life to promoting the cause of peace and understanding.

A complex and somewhat contradictory personality, then. Someone who was, perhaps, shaped by the tragedies in his life – his parents' failed marriage, the death of his mother when he was a teenager. One of John's great assets was his often-brutal honesty, which sometimes bordered on self-flagellation. But this could also be a liability.

Consider, for instance, how his son must've felt when reading the following: 'Ninety per cent of the people on this planet were born out of a bottle of whisky … All of us were Saturday-night specials. Julian's in the majority. Sean is a planned child, and therein lies the difference.'

John always had a barely concealed anger within him that would often emerge as cynical sarcasm, and he could be both funny and devastatingly nasty (sometimes simultaneously). It's there in many interviews and in all of his best songs – even ostensibly tender ones. The sound of a man struggling with inner demons, sometimes emerging triumphant but, even when he failed, still having the ability to make people snigger awkwardly.

It's been (erroneously) suggested that John's childhood was spent in a repressive environment from which his music was the only escape. That's garbage. 'I only got one beating from Mimi for taking money from her handbag,' he told Hunter Davies.

Indeed, John seems to have been a mischievous and cunning little boy. 'The sort of gang I led went in for shoplifting and pulling girls' knickers down. When the bomb fell and everyone got caught, I was always the one they missed.'

Some of the things he said (particularly in the early 70s) were contradictory, bitter and, occasionally, deliberately hurtful to friends and family. Yet, for all that, there are people – serious people, too – who elevate John to quasi-sainthood. Why?

Probably, it's because his heart was usually – and often in spite of himself – in the right place. That's why he inspired such love and devotion from those who knew him best.

For those who think Lennon could be an uncaring bastard, have a look at the TV footage of him being interviewed moments after learning of Brian Epstein's death – *that* is the real John Lennon at his most naked and vulnerable.

John's main contribution to mankind, however, wasn't as an orator on the world's problems, or as a caustic observer of its many ironies (although he did both jobs pretty well). Rather, it was as a writer of some of the most perfect pop music ever created.

He was less naturally melodically gifted than his partner, but, in some ways, that made Lennon's songs even more remarkable than McCartney's. John wrote from his soul and from a heart that he wore, all too frequently, on his sleeve.

The contradictions continue to pile up: alone among the Beatles, John cultivated relationships on the radical political left, yet he voted Tory because he felt his taxes were too high. He always regarded the Beatles as, fundamentally, *his* band yet he was the first to play outside the group (appearing on *The Rolling Stones' Rock 'n' Roll Circus* in December 1968).

After the Beatles' break-up, John spent the early 70s involved in a public slanging match with Paul that spilled over into their music and was only resolved after John had written 'How Do You Sleep?' – one of the most powerful pieces of invective ever set to music. You always sensed with John, however, that he was as quick to attempt to mend fences as he was to burn bridges.

He settled down in New York, with Yoko and Sean, and seemed content during his 'house-husband' period, although his final work – *Double Fantasy* – was disappointingly middle-of-the-road.

His murder, in 1980, not only shocked the world but was, in many ways, a final nail in the coffin for many of the things the Beatles, and Lennon himself, had symbolised. The dream really *was* over.

Ironically, in one of his final interviews, when asked what his dream for the 1980s was, John's advice to people was to 'make your own dream … You have to do it yourself.'

The 'Me generation' promptly took him at his word.

WE ALL WANNA CHANGE THE WORLD
– The Beatles' LPs

A Hard Day's Night (1964)

The first LP composed entirely of Lennon/McCartney songs, *A Hard Day's Night* was recorded between 29 January and 2 June 1964 (the sessions also produced the *Long Tall Sally* EP).

A Hard Day's Night is an often-overlooked gem next to some of the band's later works. Besides two hit singles (the title song and 'Can't Buy Me Love') it includes some of their most introspective and personal songs ('If I Fell', 'Things We Said Today') and adventurous musical experiments (the sublime 'I'll Be Back').

Given that the LP was, by design, a film soundtrack, it's even more remarkable that it includes so few fillers. 'I'll Cry Instead' shows the band's first flirtations with country music (Ringo's influence, chiefly), while 'And I Love Her' provided every bad folk trio in the land with three new chords to play with.

More acoustic and musically varied than *With The Beatles*, *A Hard Day's Night* has many claims to being the definitive early-Beatles sound.

A generation of bands based entire careers on the ringing Rickenbacker-drenched guitars and block harmonies of *A Hard Day's Night*. It's an LP that says to everyone working in a factory, or an office, or sitting in class at school: 'You can do that, or you can do *this*.' Millions were inspired and chose to do the latter.

NOTHING IS REAL
Fictionalised versions of the Beatles' story

Movies

◉ *The Birth of the Beatles* (1979)

Hilariously awful US made-for-TV biopic (on which Pete Best was technical advisor). John Altman (*EastEnders'* Nick Cotton) as George Harrison! Nigel Havers as George Martin! So bad, it's brilliant.

◉ *John and Yoko: A Love Story* (1985)

Decent TV-movie version of Sandor Stern's play, with Mark McGann reprising his stage role as Lennon, and made with the co-operation of Yoko. Interesting performance by Peter Capaldi as a tough, assertive McCartney.

◉ *The Hours and the Times* (1991)

Impressive, minimalist black-and-white art movie depicting a fictionalised (unless anyone knows different) account of Lennon and Brian Epstein's 1963 Barcelona sojourn. Fine performances from Ian Hart and David Angus.

◉ *Secrets* (aka *One Crazy Night*, 1992)

A sweet little Australian film about five teenage Beatle fans who try to smuggle into the band's Sydney hotel in 1964 and get stuck in the basement – missing the concert for which they all have tickets as a consequence. Of interest for early roles by Noah Taylor (*Almost Famous*) and Dannii Minogue and some very amusing press-conference footage featuring the Beatles themselves.

◉ *Backbeat* (1994)

Ian Softley's movie about the Beatles' Hamburg days. The main story – Stu falling for Astrid – is somewhat lightweight, but the real meat is in the period colour and excellent soundtrack. Hart effortlessly reprises his Lennon role from *The Hours and the Times* and both Gary Bakewell and Chris O'Neill are scarily good as Paul and George respectively.

Television

○ *The Rutles: All You Need is Cash* (1978)

OK, it's not *about* the Beatles per se (yeah, right) but it's still a work of unparalleled genius; Eric Idle's script and Neil Innes's songs perfectly parody the Beatles' story, full of outrageous in-jokes. Available on DVD; if you haven't got a copy, you *need* one.

○ *Everyman: John Lennon – A Journey in the Life* (1985)

Excellent, impressionistic account of John's life, featuring a great performance by Bernard Hill. Lots of musical interludes including Roy Orbison singing 'Help!'

○ *Alas, Smith and Jones* (1988)

A five-minute sketch from the (usually smug) UK comedy duo that brilliantly parodied the *Making of Sgt. Pepper's* documentary. Full of inventive song fragments with hilarious lyrics (sample: 'The evening sounds incredibly dull, so I will spend it out of me skull round George's place').

Books

○ *Paperback Writer* (1978)

Mark Shipper's terrific 'alternative history' of the Beatles, complete with sharp, clever in-jokes. Some of the Americanisms deflate the overall effect, but the final chapters, as the Beatles re-form for a predictably disastrous tour on the same bill as the Sex Pistols, are worth their weight in comedy gold.

SHE SAID SHE SAID
Quotes (part 1)

Prior to the Beatles' success, most pop stars had behaved like the proverbial good children — seen, but not heard. Even the more articulate ones tended to keep their gobs shut in public for fear of generating negative publicity. The Beatles' mixture of bravado and wit changed all that and, in the process, opened up an entirely new school of thought on what issues were relevant for a musician to talk about.

They charmed the world's press with their pithy comebacks to — let's be fair — often downright inane questions and, generally, had a right good laugh at the expense of others. But they did it in such a way that kept the hacks coming back for more. Here's a sample of the comedy diamonds that would routinely emerge from the average interview.

- In Australia, John strenuously denied that the Beatles were millionaires. When asked what, therefore, happened to all the money they made, he noted that most went to Her Majesty. '*She's* a millionaire,' added George.

- Ringo, asked why he wore two rings on each finger: 'Because I can't fit them through me nose.'

- John, when asked if he had any explanation why the reporter himself had been attacked by girl fans because they believed he'd met the Beatles: 'Well, you're lovely to look at.'

- George, when told that the Beatles' tour plane would be fitted with rope ladders in the event of emergencies: 'I presume we won't be flying more than six feet off the ground?'

- John, replying to a reporter's incredulity that the Beatles didn't rehearse their own songs: 'We wrote 'em, we recorded 'em, we play 'em every day. What do you rehearse?'

- Ringo, having expressed surprise at the sunshine of Miami, is asked if they don't have sunny days in Liverpool. 'No, they've finished up there.'

Do You Want to Know a Secret?

⊙ Paul, when told that a group of Detroit students had started a 'Stamp Out Beatles' campaign: 'We're gonna start a campaign to stamp out Detroit.'

⊙ George, asked if he had any suggestions for possible American repayments to England for giving them the Beatles: 'Just let us off with our income tax.'

⊙ John, asked from where his hairdo came: 'Out of me scalp.'

⊙ Ringo, when asked how he would like to be remembered: 'I'd just like to end up as sort of unforgettable.'

ROLL OVER BEETHOVEN
Real people in Beatles songs

⊙ Ludwig van Beethoven (1770–1827): German symphonic composer and famous, apparently. Appears (naturally) in 'Roll Over Beethoven' as does …

⊙ Pyotr Ilyich Tchaikovsky (1840–93): Russian composer of *The Nutcracker* and *Swan Lake*.

⊙ Edward Lear (1812–88): English artist, humorist and author of *Nonsense Songs*. Mentioned in 'Paperback Writer'.

⊙ Harold Wilson (1916–95): British Prime Minister 1964–70 and 1974–76. His government's fiscal policy inspired 'Taxman'.

⊙ Edward Heath (b. 1916): British Prime Minister 1970–74. Leader of the Opposition at the time of his namecheck in 'Taxman'.

⊙ Robert Freyman (1906–87): New York psychiatrist to the stars. The probable inspiration for 'Dr Robert'.

⊙ Pablo Fanques (1796–1871): Victorian travelling-circus owner whose company included tightrope-walker William Kite and trampoline-gymnasts John and Agnes Henderson. A poster advertising a performance by the troupe, on the Town Meadows, Rochdale in 1843, inspired 'Being For The Benefit Of Mr Kite'. And a splendid time *was* guaranteed for all.

⊙ Edgar Allan Poe (1809–49): American poet and author of stories of the macabre. Kicked by elementary penguins in 'I Am The Walrus'.

⊙ Mao Tse-tung (1893–1976): Chinese revolutionary leader, politician and mass murderer. Cited as being not very groovy in 'Revolution'.

⊙ Prudence Farrow: The sister of Mia Farrow who accompanied the Beatles to Rishikesh in 1968. Prudence threw herself into meditation and, seemingly, somewhat overdid it, inspiring 'Dear Prudence'.

⊙ Paul McCartney (b. 1942): Mentioned in 'Glass Onion'.

Do You Want to Know a Secret?

- Sir Walter Raleigh (1552–1618): Elizabethan privateer and explorer. Introduced the potato and tobacco to Britain. Concerning the latter, he is described as 'a stupid git' in 'I'm So Tired'.

- Bob Dylan (b. 1941): American singer/songwriter. His 1965 song 'Ballad Of A Thin Man' is referenced in 'Yer Blues'.

- Peter Brown: NEMS employee and the best man at John Lennon's wedding in 1969. Namechecked in 'The Ballad Of John And Yoko'.

- BB King (b.1925): Blues guitarist mentioned in 'Dig It'.

- Doris Day (b. 1924): American singer and actress best known for *Calamity Jane* (1953). Mentioned in 'Dig It'.

- Matt Busby (1909–94): Scottish international footballer and, subsequently, manager of Manchester United 1945–69. Namechecked in 'Dig It'.

YOU CAN'T DO THAT
Unusual instruments heard on Beatles records

- Ringo's percussion on 'Words Of Love' was obtained by him slapping a suitcase.

- Paul played a clavichord on 'For No One'.

- George used a svarmandal (an Indian zither) on 'Strawberry Fields Forever'.

- There's a glockenspiel featured on 'Only A Northern Song', though sources differ as to who played it. Paul plays the trumpet.

- The clavioline – a French monophonic keyboard previously best known for its use on the Tornados' 'Telstar'. Played by John on 'Baby, You're A Rich Man'.

- 'All Together Now' features John on ukulele. Many years later, George would also play the instrument, in George Formby-style, on 'Free As A Bird'.

- The banjo was the first instrument that John learned (taught by his mother when he was a teenager). He finally got to play one on 'All You Need Is Love'.

- The distinctive recorder solo on 'The Fool On The Hill' was played by Paul, who also briefly reprised it on 'Glass Onion'.

- 'Helter Skelter' was the product of a completely mad session, not least of which was John Lennon honking away on saxophone.

- Paul's instrumental versatility was further demonstrated when he played flugelhorn on 'Dear Prudence'.

- For 'I Will' the percussion was a combination of Ringo on bongos and John tapping out the beat with a drumstick on something metal (possibly a tin box).

⊙ George purchased his Moog synthesizer in California in November 1968 and used it on his second solo LP *Electronic Sounds* (recorded February 1969 – the Moog had first appeared on the Monkees 1967 LP *Pisces, Aquarius, Capricorn, Jones*). Set up in Room 43 at EMI, it became *the* key sound on *Abbey Road*. John used it on 'I Want You (She's So Heavy)', Paul on 'Maxwell's Silver Hammer' and George played it on 'Oh! Darling', 'Octopus's Garden', 'Because' and – most memorably – 'Here Comes The Sun'.

⊙ Amid the ringing arpeggioed guitars on 'You Never Give Me Your Money', Paul is also playing wind chimes.

WE ALL WANNA CHANGE THE WORLD
– The Beatles' LPs

Beatles For Sale (1964)

Most commentators regard *Beatles For Sale* as a somewhat tired collection of songs and a (possibly unconscious) sign that the strain of Beatlemania was beginning to show. Certainly some of John and Paul's lyrics were much darker and more morose than the sun-bright compositions on *A Hard Day's Night* (see 'No Reply', 'I'm A Loser', 'Baby's In Black').

Recorded between 11 August and 26 October 1964, the presence of a bunch of hastily recorded covers (most of them done – in very few takes – on 18 October) suggests a lack of obvious creativity. The fact that the two best songs from the sessions – Lennon's pop classic 'I Feel Fine' and McCartney's impressively in-your-face 'She's A Woman' – were paired as a stand-alone single didn't help.

And quite why a furious version of Little Willie John's 'Leave My Kitten Alone' stayed locked in the archives until 1995 in favour of less successful covers ('Mr Moonlight', 'Everybody's Trying To Be My Baby') is a question that only the Beatles and George Martin can answer.

Nevertheless, ignoring all of the above, any LP that features 'No Reply', 'Eight Days A Week' and 'Every Little Thing' can't be *all* bad. There are also two of their best covers, 'Kansas City' and 'Rock And Roll Music'. Indeed, in terms of the Beatles' overall sound, *Beatles For Sale* saw the band's first hesitant steps towards the studio trickery that they would subsequently master.

They *do* look like they could use some sleep on the sleeve photograph, however.

I SHOULD HAVE KNOWN BETTER
Urban myths and fallacies concerning the Beatles

Over the years so many books and articles have been written about the Beatles that, inevitably, the odd inaccuracy has been published, gone uncorrected and has gone on to become accepted as fact.

These, along with a variety of long-held myths, still crop up occasionally when some journalist, unfamiliar with the minutiae of the band, is putting together a feature. Here is a sample of them.

The Beatles were working-class bruisers from the council estates

A common misconception during the 60s, not exactly helped by Lennon writing a song called 'Working Class Hero'.

The common belief was that the Beatles were four lads from rough inner-city Liverpool, not particularly well educated and at least two of whom came from what used to be called 'broken homes'. Only Ringo really fits this stereotypical profile. The other three were all grammar-school boys.

Paul's was a two-income family (until his mother died when he was fourteen), a rarity in 1950s Britain. John, raised by an aunt and uncle who owned their own business in suburban Woolton, was most definitely middle class.

John Lennon was born as Luftwaffe bombs fell on Liverpool

Well, he said he was several times. Hunter Davies and Philip Norman both mentioned this in their biographies. Sadly, it's not true. There was no air raid over the city on 9 October 1940.

John thought up the name Beatles

As early as July 1961 John was claiming authorship of the band's name, via quasi-divine inspiration, in an amusing *Goon Show*-style article for *MerseyBeat*.

Leaving aside men on flaming pies for a second, a more serious Lennon suggestion was that the name derived from Buddy Holly's backing group, the Crickets. When people heard the name, they thought of insects, but when they saw it written down (with an 'a') it was obviously a reference to beat music.

However, most Beatles historians now conclude that it was actually Stu Sutcliffe who devised the name in 1960 – initially 'the Beatals', then 'the Silver Beetles' – possibly (although some evidence suggests otherwise) taken from the name of the biker gang's girlfriends in the film *The Wild Ones*.

George Martin signed the Beatles because they made him laugh

One of the most oft-told Beatle stories concerns their audition for EMI on 6 June 1962. Having been somewhat unimpressed with their musical efforts, George Martin asked if there was anything that the band had problems with. To which George Harrison replied, 'I don't like your tie.'

Martin, showing the sense of humour to be expected from someone who had shared a studio with Spike Milligan and Peter Sellers, elected to see the funny side, liked the Beatles' irreverent wit and signed them as much for that reason as any musical ability.

Great story. Unfortunately it ignores the fact that the Beatles' first three-year contract with EMI had been agreed by Brian Epstein and Martin in May, over a month before Martin even met the Beatles.

Some bloke called Andy White, rather than Ringo, plays drums on 'Love Me Do'

Well, he did and he didn't. The Beatles second session at Abbey Road – their first with Ringo in the drum-seat – on 4 September 1962 produced versions of 'Love Me Do' and 'How Do You Do It?' both, at that stage, under consideration for the band's first 45.

George Martin, however, decided that he'd like another go at recording 'Love Me Do' and, a week later, the Beatles trooped back to London to find session drummer Andy White sitting in with them. Ringo played tambourine.

In the end, however, it was the 4 September version of 'Love Me Do' that became the band's first single – released in October.

At some stage during the next few months, the master tape of this was mislaid. Thus, when the *Please Please Me* LP was being compiled, the Andy White version of 'Love Me Do' was used instead.

Ringo, incidentally, *didn't* play drums on 'Love Me Do's B-side, 'PS I Love You'. That song, also recorded on 11 September, features White, with Ringo on maracas.

John was the rocker, Paul the balladeer

A common misconception, partly down to Lennon's tough image and bolshiness in interviews and also, at least in part, because of some of the mawkish, annoying 'silly love songs' that Macca put out in the 1970s.

A simple listen to 'This Boy', 'If I Fell' and 'Julia' on the one hand and 'I'm Down', 'Helter Skelter' and 'The End' on the other should put paid to that myth.

Fifty-fifty Lennon/McCartney collaborations ended after 1963

Again, this was something that Lennon said in several interviews after the Beatles broke up. McCartney's biography, *Many Years From Now*, put a completely different spin on the accepted wisdom of how the pair wrote their songs.

In the early days they did, indeed, write together eyeball-to-eyeball. They wrote 'From Me To You' on a tour bus travelling from York to Shrewsbury, 'She Loves You' in a hotel room in Newcastle and 'I Want To Hold Your Hand' in the basement of the Asher residence in London. It was probably that kind of collaboration that John was referring to as having ended in 1963.

However, both John and Paul had always started songs themselves that they would then take in half or almost-completed form to their partner for suggestions and advice. According to McCartney, this process continued more or less until the end of the Beatles' career.

Thus, it's fair to suggest that even songs which are traditionally thought of as pure Lennon or McCartney compositions, had at least a bit of input from the other partner.

The Beatles said they wouldn't go to America until they had a No. 1 record

This is Paul's particular bit of myth-revisionism. He has noted on several occasions that, because the Beatles had seen UK stars like Cliff Richard struggle to make headway in the US, they told Brian Epstein they would only go to America when they had a No. 1.

A lovely story, and it's perfectly possible the Beatles did, indeed, tell Epstein something along those lines. But Brian had negotiated the Beatles' appearance on *The Ed Sullivan Show* in November 1963, a month before 'I Want To Hold Your Hand' was even released. They were flying to New York on 7 February 1964, to appear on the Sullivan show two days later, whether they were No. 1 or No. 86.

As it happens, on 18 January, while they were in Paris, the Beatles were told that the single had reached No. 1 in the American charts.

The Beatles smoked pot in the Buckingham Palace loos as they waited to get their MBEs

Lennon claimed that they did in 1970, a comment which brought a predictably rabid response from the tabloid press. This would seem to have been one of John's regular media wind-ups, as both Harrison and McCartney vehemently denied doing any such thing.

The Beatles once jammed with Elvis

The Beatles as a group met Elvis Presley just once, at his home on Perugia Way in Bel-Air on 27 August 1965. The meeting was set up by a *New Musical Express* journalist, Chris Hutchins, who would eventually write a book about it (*Elvis and the Beatles*). The Beatles attended, along with their entourage – Neil Aspinall, Mal Evans, Alf Bicknell and Tony Barrow.

Both John and Hutchins would subsequently suggest that a jam session had taken place between them. Hutchins even detailed some of the songs that they, allegedly, performed.

In *Anthology*, Paul, Ringo and George all denied this. Respectively, they remembered that: Elvis had a Fender bass which he occasionally plucked at, Ringo played *football* with Elvis, and George had spent most of the evening trying to work out which of Elvis's friends had any reefers.

John was the only Beatle interested in the avant-garde and the emerging underground scene

After John began his collaborations with Yoko Ono and started to incorporate her ideas of performance art into his own music (with mixed, if occasionally inspired, results) it became fashionable to regard John as the experimental Beatle.

In terms of having his finger on the pulse of new ideas, however, he was often left trailing in Paul McCartney's wake. John spent most of the mid-60s living a very conventional suburban lifestyle in Weybridge.

By contrast, McCartney's home in St John's Wood gave him direct access to the capital's nightlife and arts scene, via his friendship with people like Barry Miles, John Dunbar and Robert Fraser. It's also worth remembering that, during one conversation at the Indica Gallery, Miles recalls John's observation that avant-garde was 'French for bullshit!'

George's sitar on 'Norwegian Wood' was the first Indian influence on western music

In November 1960, Peter Sellers and Sophia Loren's comedy classic 'Goodness Gracious Me' (produced by George Martin) introduced the ringing tones of the sitar to the British charts.

Granted, that *was* a novelty record. Nevertheless, the sound must have stayed in the minds of a few guitarists and both the Yardbirds' Jeff Beck and the Kinks' Ray Davies produced sitar-like effects on 'Heartful Of Soul' and 'See My Friend' respectively a full four months before *Rubber Soul* was released.

It's certainly fair to say that George's interest in the sitar helped to popularise the instrument and, when Brian Jones also got one some months later, it became a virtual permanent fixture on many band's recordings over the next two years.

John wrote eighty per cent of the lyrics of 'Eleanor Rigby'

In two interviews – with *Rolling Stone* in 1970 and *Playboy* in 1980 – Lennon claimed this (noting that it was 'Paul's baby, but I helped with the education of the child').

McCartney remembered things somewhat differently, saying that some of the lyrics were group efforts (Ringo, for example, thought up Father McKenzie darning his socks) but that John had actually contributed very little.

John's friend Pete Shotton, who was at Lennon's home when the song was composed, broadly agrees with this.

Sgt. Pepper's Lonely Hearts Club Band is the greatest record ever made by anyone

It's not even the greatest record ever made by the Beatles! Song for song, it isn't a patch on either *Revolver* or *Rubber Soul*. *Sgt. Pepper's* is a beautifully produced record, with time and care having been lavished upon it, but it's a flawed work, nonetheless.

As early as 1974, doubts were being cast upon the widely held belief that it was an unsurpassed masterpiece, Charles Shaar Murray in the *NME* calling it 'the point where rock and roll almost OD'ed on itself'.

Even the Beatles themselves had their doubts. George regarded it as 'of its time'. Ringo's main memory was learning to play chess during its making. And, while Paul still clearly has fond memories of the album, John's assessment was, possibly, the most accurate: 'It worked cos we said it worked.'

Stereo Please Please Me LPs are worth £3,000

Periodically, when they haven't got anything else to publish, one of the tabloids may do an article on record collecting. Inevitably, this will include a list of the ten rarest records in the world and, alongside the Pistols' 'God Save The Queen' on A&M and other legendary rare records, will be a statement that stereo copies of the Beatles first LP are worth megabucks.

What usually happens thereafter is that a few gullible people will search through their vinyl, find they have a stereo copy of *Please Please Me* (which they bought for a fiver in the mid-80s) and rush to their local second-hand record shop only to be told that what they've got is worth a couple of quid, if that.

Records (particularly the successful ones) used to remain on catalogue for long periods but, every so often, a new batch would be pressed up with a slight amendment to either the cover, or the label, or both.

So, for anyone who thinks they may have a valuable item gathering dust in the cupboard, please note: the – very rare – *Please Please Me* variant to which this price tag refers is one that was available, for a short time only, in early 1963 when almost all records sold were mono rather than stereo.

It can be easily identified by its black label, which features distinctive gold lettering. *Not* the subsequent black with yellow lettering, or black with silver lettering, both of which are common as muck.

It's also worth noting that this price refers to a record in mint condition. Chances are if you bought *Please Please Me* in 1963, you'll have played it a few times since. Each time you put the stylus on the record, you're diminishing any potential resale value.

Finally, a word of advice to all would-be record collectors. Remember, any record is only 'worth' what someone else is prepared to pay for it. In strictly scrap-value terms what you've actually got is twelve inches of black plastic housed in a cardboard sleeve. The raw materials are worth no more than a penny.

After leaving Rishikesh, the Beatles had nothing further to do with the Maharishi

The Beatles brief-but-infamous flirtation with Indian guru the Maharishi Mahesh Yogi, which flourished during the later part of 1967, came to an abrupt end on 12 April 1968.

John, George and their wives left the swami's spiritual retreat after an alleged incident was reported (supposedly by their friend Alex Mardas) that the Maharishi had attempted to sexually exploit one of his female initiates. (John subsequently suggested the woman in question was the actress Mia Farrow, though this remains unconfirmed.)

John was especially bitter to discover that his idol had feet of clay and wrote 'Sexy Sadie' by way of therapy.

Although there has always been some sniggering at any mention of the Maharishi's name in connection with the Beatles, both Cynthia Lennon and McCartney have subsequently written that they believe the Maharishi was the victim of a smear campaign.

George eventually returned to the guru's fold and, during the 1990s, raised money for the Natural Law Party, the political wing of the Maharishi's organisation.

If you play 'Revolution 9' backwards, it contains Satanic messages or evidence that Paul is dead

On the contrary, if you play 'Revolution 9' (or, indeed, any other record) backwards, the most that you're likely to encounter is a bunch of random gibberish and, possibly, a broken stylus.

George temporarily quit the Beatles in 1969 after an argument with Paul

Luridly captured in the *Let It Be* movie is the moment at Twickenham where the Beatles are rehearsing 'Two Of Us' and McCartney tells Harrison how to play the solo.

'I'll play what you want me to play,' says George, miserably. 'Or I won't play at all if you don't want me to.' For more than twenty years everyone involved, including all four Beatles, remembered this as the moment that George decided enough was enough, quit the band, went home to Esher and wrote 'Wah Wah' to convey his feelings.

That is, until the release of Sulpy and Schweighardt's *Get Back: the Unauthorised Chronicle of the Beatles Let It Be Disaster* in 1997. Having studied every available audiotape from January 1969, they made a startling discovery.

The argument with Paul occurred on 6 January, but George didn't walk out until four days later. And, when he did, it was actually after a lengthy argument with John. (Contemporary press reports confirm this, along with John's – apparently serious – suggestion that if George didn't return by the next week, they should replace him with Eric Clapton.)

There's no doubt that in January 1969, George Harrison was a deeply unhappy man. Having just spent seven weeks in the relaxed environment of California producing Jackie Lomax's *Is This What You Want?* and then hanging out with the Band and Bob Dylan in Woodstock, George returned to London to find himself in the middle of what he would subsequently describe as 'the winter of discontent'.

He was especially depressed by constantly having his songs belittled by John and Paul. (Considering that both 'All Things Must Pass' and 'Isn't It A Pity' were tried out during these sessions but rejected in favour of – clearly inferior – Lennon and McCartney songs, who could, honestly, blame him?)

John, meanwhile, had two important new elements in his life – Yoko Ono and heroin. Neither of which made communicating with him very easy. Paul, as ever, was simply trying to keep the band together – he argues as much in the movie. But he was getting on everybody's tits doing so.

It appears, from the evidence of Sulpy and Schweighardt's book, that it was John's unwillingness to engage in rational communication that was the final straw for

Do You Want to Know a Secret?

George. Which leaves one question unanswered. Why was Paul content to play the fall guy for this situation for so long?

The last Beatles song recorded was 'Golden Slumbers'

This often reported 'fact' appears to have first cropped up in a fan publication in the mid-70s, when details of the Beatles' studio recordings were still shrouded in mystery. It continues to appear every now and then on the Internet.

'Golden Slumbers' – and its companion piece 'Carry That Weight' – were recorded on 2 July 1969, towards the start of the *Abbey Road* sessions. Some further overdubs were carried out on the song later in the month, with the final recordings taking place on 15 August.

The last song to be started on *Abbey Road* was 'Because', recorded between 1 and 5 August. Overdubs then continued for the next couple of weeks, with the final batch being completed on 18 August (including the orchestration for 'The End'). That day was, almost certainly, the last time that all four Beatles were together in the studio at the same time.

However, the last actual Beatles recording (before the mid-90s, anyway) occurred on 3 and 4 January 1970 when Paul, George and Ringo recorded 'I Me Mine' and some overdubs for 'Let It Be'. John was in Denmark at the time, having already told his colleagues that he'd left the band.[2]

Yoko was responsible for the Beatles breaking-up

Arguably, the Beatles began to break up the moment that Brian Epstein died. 'I really didn't have any misconceptions about our ability to do anything other than play music,' Lennon noted in 1970. 'I was scared, I thought, "We've f*ckin' had it."'

That they remained together for a further two years was testimony to the significant bond that existed between them. During that time they made some genuinely great music, squabbled, made a couple of films, squabbled, started their own record label and squabbled.

---

[2] Technically, the final Beatle recording session took place on 1 April 1970, when the Phil Spector-produced overdubs for the *Let It Be* LP were cut. But, since Ringo was the only Beatle taking part, that doesn't really count.

But they weren't little boys any more, they'd grown up and the glue that held them together was beginning to come unstuck. Yoko simply had the misfortune to fall in love with John at the very moment when he was – perhaps unconsciously – searching for a new direction in his life.

Due to Jeff Lynne's influence 'Free As A Bird' sounds, musically, like ELO

Actually, it doesn't – there are no cellos for a start. Arguably, if it had, it would have sounded *more* like the Beatles than what we ended up with. Indeed, what 'Free As A Bird' most resembles is a George Harrison solo track, especially the trademark slide-guitar.

The Walrus was Paul

Despite what John assured us in 'Glass Onion', no, he wasn't. John himself was.

I'M LOOKING THROUGH YOU
Paul McCartney – a portrait of the artist as a young man

It was hard to believe when he was singing 'We All Stand Together' with the Frog Chorus (or involved in those depressingly twee collaborations with Stevie Wonder and Michael Jackson) but, for a few years in the mid-60s, if Paul McCartney wasn't the most talented man on the planet he was in the top two. Someone who wrote effortlessly inventive pop classics as easily as most people drew breath.

Yet, for some reason, while Paul was always loved (he was, after all 'the pretty one'), he was never really admired as much as he should have been. Philip Norman's *Shout!* suggests a few potential reasons. Macca was often seen by both the media and the public as the PR man in the Beatles, the manipulator, the one who rewrote history as easily as he wrote great songs.

Certainly, if you see that interview the fresh-faced, butter-wouldn't-melt Paul gave to *The Mersey Sound* in 1963, when he noted that the Beatles gave up their leathers because they didn't want to be seen as 'a gang of idiots', it induces a slightly sick feeling in the stomach.

Many of the 'crimes' that Paul is often charged with – being an overt sentimentalist, a spin-doctor, a social climber, a gadfly – are either grossly unfair or, even if true, they're hardly the worst of sins. That a kid from the council estates of Liverpool ended up not only getting knighted, but also as one of the richest men in the world, might be down to *some* of the above, but it was, mostly, because of hard work and astonishing talent.

Those who meet Paul tend to come away impressed. When one of the next generation of Liverpool bands, the Teardrop Explodes, shared AIR studios with McCartney in 1982, Julian Cope noted that he'd expected to *hate* Paul. Instead, Cope found himself charmed and rather tongue-tied having talked to a living legend.

In recent years we've discovered that Paul was the Beatle who first got into making experimental home tapes; the social Beatle who got invited to all the best nightclubs and groovy parties; the one who was the last to take acid, but the first to take cocaine. In the 1965–67 period, Paul McCartney was bang at the heart of *everything* that was going on in the emergent psychedelic, underground scene, which was famously documented in Peter Whitehead's film *Tonite, Let's All Make Love in London.*

Yet he still wasn't the 'cool' Beatle. That was always John. Maybe it was because for every 'Here, There And Everywhere' or 'Hey Jude' there was also a 'Maxwell's Silver Hammer' or an 'Ob-La-Di, Ob-La-Da' lurking in the McCartney songbook.

Macca's love of 1920s and 1930s popular music was something he inherited from his dad, a dance-band pianist. It was also something he shared (to an extent, anyway) with both Lennon and Harrison. But sometimes Paul would push for perfection in form, to the exclusion of substance, something that could infuriate his colleagues.

When Ian MacDonald described McCartney, post-1967, as the Beatles 'de facto musical director' he had a point. Paul, as he is proud to acknowledge, *was* coming up with lots of concepts during this period (both *Sgt. Pepper's* and *The Magical Mystery Tour* were, essentially, McCartney ideas).

Subsequently, both John and George would complain about Paul's insistence on spending hours getting his own compositions *just so* but, by contrast, having a more experimental attitude towards the work of others. Yet McCartney's bass-playing is one of the Beatles real undiscovered treasures – effortless melodic lines that sound like a frustrated guitarist.

After *Abbey Road*, Paul spent a few years trying to get anywhere near that level of creativity again. He sort of made it with *Band On The Run* though, to be honest, Wings were little more than a good singles band.

Having staggered, uninspired, through the 80s, McCartney rediscovered himself in the 90s, first as a live act (his 1993 world tour was one of the biggest grossing in history) and then as a kind of grandfather figure to the Britpop movement.

He started releasing good records again (*Flaming Pie, Run Devil Run*) and though he cruelly lost Linda, his prop for three decades, he entered the new millennium remarried and as a father again at the age of sixty.

When asked about how he viewed watching his own past in *Anthology*, Paul replied,'It was a bit shocking to see my personality so clearly portrayed ... "God in heaven, what is he *on*?"'

The world's most famous vegetarian, a Renaissance man for the twenty-first century (painter, poet, classical composer), his triumphant performance at the Glastonbury Festival in 2004 — playing 'Helter Skelter' live for the first time — was a reminder of what no amount of spin can change. That Sir Paul McCartney, MBE, wrote some good tunes in his day.

ONLY A NORTHERN SONG
Parochial references in Beatles lyrics

Although America took them completely to their hearts, the Beatles were proud of their English (and specifically *Northern* English) roots. Many of their songs include allusions to aspects of life and culture that may have confused their overseas fans:

Daily Mail

Conservative, opinionated tabloid newspaper, mentioned in 'Paperback Writer'. It was Lennon and McCartney's daily rag of choice during the mid-60s. Two stories in the *Mail* on 17 January 1967 (one concerning the inquest into the death of Tara Browne, the heir to the Guinness fortune who was killed when he crashed his car, and the other about potholes in Blackburn) would inspire the lyrics of 'A Day In The Life'. Another story, about teenage runaway Melanie Coe, which appeared on 27 February 1967, was the basis for 'She's Leaving Home'.

The National Health Service

First introduced in 1946. Referred to in 'Dr Robert'.

Remembrance Day

Held annually on the Sunday closest to 11 November to commemorate the dead of two world wars. Hinted at by the nurse who is 'selling poppies from a tray' in 'Penny Lane'.

Meet the Wife

A rather awful BBC sitcom starring Thora Hird and Freddie Frinton, which ran for 39 episodes (28 December 1963 to 19 December 1966). Referred to in 'Good Morning, Good Morning'.

Do You Want to Know a Secret?

The House of Lords

The upper chamber of Britain's parliament, composed of peers of the realm. Referenced in 'A Day In The Life'.

Yellow matter custard

The opening line of a — really disgusting — schoolyard chant that Lennon borrowed for 'I Am The Walrus'.

The National Trust

An organisation concerned with the preservation of historic buildings. Mentioned in 'Happiness Is A Warm Gun'. Many years later, John's childhood home would be, like the soap impression of the woman in this song, donated to the National Trust.

Tea

Referred to in both 'Good Morning, Good Morning' and 'It's All Too Much'. Not a cuppa, but rather the meal (usually eaten around 5–6 p.m.) after work.

Ten bob note

A pre-decimal banknote for ten shillings (equivalent to 50 pence these days). What 'Mean Mr Mustard' kept up his nose.

The *News of the World*

A somewhat salacious Sunday tabloid newspaper. 'Polythene Pam' was the kind of girl who appeared in it.

BBC

Began radio broadcasts in 1922 and introduced the world's first high-definition television service in 1936. Mentioned in 'Dig It'.

WE ALL WANNA CHANGE THE WORLD
– The Beatles' LPs

Help! (1965)

Well, it's got two *great* singles on it ('Ticket To Ride' and the title song). Three if you count the American-only No. 1 'Yesterday'. There's also 'You're Gonna Lose That Girl' and 'You've Got To Hide Your Love Away', two beautiful performances. But elsewhere, *Help!* is a rather ordinary collection of some pretty unexceptional songs.

Conventional wisdom is that the Beatles were, creatively, lost in a sea of pot around this time. The fact that the *Help!* sessions – 15 February to 17 June 1965 – produced not only the fourteen songs on the LP but also two B-sides ('Yes It Is' and 'I'm Down'), a song that was only initially released in America ('Bad Boy'), one they left for their next LP ('Wait') and two that remained unreleased for three decades ('That Means A Lot' and 'If You've Got Troubles') suggests otherwise. Although, as at least one review of *Anthology 2* noted, 'If You've Got Troubles' is not only the worst song ever sung, it's the worst song ever sung … by Ringo Starr.

Many of the songs on *Help!* seem directionless, with trite lyrics ('It's Only Love') or clichéd sentiments ('You Like Me Too Much'). Musically, there is a certain amount of experimentation going on but there's a suspicion that when the Beatles discovered a new toy around this period (the volume tone-pedal, for instance), they'd use it to the point of boredom.

How ironic that such an innovative film should have such a lightweight soundtrack LP.

EVERY LITTLE THING
Twenty strange-but-true facts

1. One would imagine that the innovative 'She Said She Said' was always held in high regard by Beatle-people. Not so. In October 1966, in a poll in *The Beatles Monthly*, the song was voted 'least favourite' on *Revolver* by the readership.

2. On 18 May 1968, John Lennon called a meeting at Apple's offices at 95 Wigmore Street to inform his surprised colleagues that he was, in fact, the reincarnation of Jesus Christ. The meeting broke up shortly afterwards so that Paul, George and Ringo could process this information.

3. Paul – along with his friend Tara Browne – spent Christmas 1965 at the home of Paul's father in Cheshire. On Boxing Day, while messing about on their mopeds, Paul crashed. He chipped his tooth and sustained a nasty cut on his top lip, which required stitches.

As it happens, the Beatles didn't make any public appearances for several months thereafter, so the scar had plenty of time to heal (although Paul's tooth still hadn't been capped five months later when they made the promo film for 'Paperback Writer'). Subsequently, this incident became a vital part of the notorious 'Paul is Dead' myth.

4. An example of the way memory can cheat even those involved: McCartney has remembered in several interviews that he played Bob Dylan an early copy of *Sgt. Pepper's* at the Mayfair Hotel, London, in the company of Keith Richards. Dylan's response was, 'I get it, you don't want to be cute any more.'

When questioned as to whether *Revolver* wasn't the LP in question, Macca has insisted that, no, it was definitely *Sgt. Pepper's*. In reality, it was *Revolver*. Paul, together with Richards and Brian Jones, visited Dylan's hotel suite during the afternoon of 27 May 1966. (Later that evening, John and George watched Dylan and the Hawks' apocalyptic performance at the Royal Albert Hall. The next day John was filmed with Dylan driving from Weybridge to London in DA Pennebaker's documentary, *Eat the Document*.)

5. John professed absolute distaste for Paul's 20s-style charmer 'Honey Pie' in 1980 ('I don't even want to *think* about that'). Ironic, then, that the Django Reinhardt-influenced guitar solo was, it seems, the work of John Lennon. It was considered 'brilliant' by George in a 1987 interview.

6. Though they were often accused of hiding meanings within their songs, on the odd occasion when the Beatles *did* indulge in a bit of cheeky innuendo, most people missed it. Case in point: How the hell did they get away with 'Girl', a song that includes allusions to sadomasochism, deliberate double entendre and very obvious heavy breathing (as well as Paul and George singing 'tit' over and over in the background)?

7. So nervous were EMI by the potential to be sued by the people whose photos were used on Peter Blake's elaborate *Sgt. Pepper's* cover montage that they insisted the Beatles contact all those still living and obtain written permission.

All agreed except actor Leo Gorcey, who wanted $500. As a consequence, his image was airbrushed out (he should have been next to Huntz Hall). Also removed was Mahatma Gandhi, at EMI's insistence (his position would have been between Lewis Carroll and Diana Dors).

Those who *do* feature include Aleister Crowley, Carl Jung, Bob Dylan, Edgar Allan Poe, Aldous Huxley, Laurel and Hardy, Karl Marx, Marlon Brando, Oscar Wilde, George Bernard Shaw, HG Wells, Fred Astaire, Marilyn Monroe and Liverpool footballer Albert Stubbins.

8. The harmonica that John used on 'Love Me Do' was, almost certainly, one that he'd shoplifted in Arnhem, when the Beatles were en route to Hamburg in August 1960.

9. In December 1963, the *Daily Mail* ran a story that the Beatles were supporting an Oxfam campaign to raise a million pounds for world hunger. In actual fact they had merely been photographed holding collecting tins and a poster provided by a young man involved (at a very low level) in the campaign. His name? Jeffrey Archer.

Some months later, the writer Sheridan Morley — then a student at Oxford — had dinner with Ringo, who told Morley that he considered Archer 'the sort of bloke who would bottle your piss and sell it'.

10. In a show of solidarity with their mates the Rolling Stones — Mick and Keith were facing drugs charges at the time — John and Paul sang backing vocals on the

Stones' epic 1967 single 'We Love You'. Their contributions were recorded on 18 May, a session also attended by poet Allen Ginsberg.

11. One of McCartney's most urbane melodies, 'Michelle', actually had its origins in a Chet Atkins-style instrumental that Paul had played at the student parties Lennon invited him to around 1960.

When another song was needed for *Rubber Soul*, John remembered the 'French thing' Paul used to perform. John wrote some of the words, having been inspired by Nina Simone's 'I Put A Spell On You', while the French lyrics were translated by Jan Vaughan, the wife of John and Paul's friend Ivan.

Musically, McCartney has noted both the influence of Bizet on the bass line (he's probably referring to *Carmen*) and a man named Jim Gretty who worked in a guitar shop in Liverpool and taught the teenage Paul and George some tricky jazz chords.

12. It's often stated that John Lennon went to school with comedian Jimmy Tarbuck and BBC newsreader Peter Sissons. All three did, indeed, attend Dovedale Primary School in the mid-40s although Tarbuck, born in February 1940, was in the school year above Lennon and Sissons (who *was* in John's class). Dovedale was also the junior school attended by George Harrison, who started there the year that John left.

13. Paul McCartney *didn't* die in a car crash in 1966 – honestly – however, the world was almost deprived of his talent three years earlier. During April 1963, while John and Brian Epstein were in Spain, Paul, George and Ringo went on holiday with Klaus Voormann and Astrid Kirchherr in Tenerife. Paul went for a swim, was caught in dangerous undercurrents and nearly drowned before managing to struggle back to shore.

14. One of the most oft-quoted fallacies concerning the Beatles relates to 'Only A Northern Song'. In an interview, *Yellow Submarine* producer Al Brodax noted that 'At two o'clock in the morning, in EMI's studio, with the London Symphony Orchestra patiently waiting to go home, we were still one song short. George told me to sit tight while he knocked out another tune. "Here Al," he said, "it's only a northern song."'

This quote, often incorrectly attributed to Harrison himself, was subsequently accepted as fact until comprehensive details of the Beatles' recordings became public in the 1980s. It was then revealed that far from being recorded in February 1968, the song was actually a year older than that.

The fact that there's clearly no orchestra playing on 'Only A Northern Song' should, perhaps, have alerted fans to the erroneous nature of this 'fact'.

15. At 5 p.m. on Wednesday 16 October 1968, John, Paul and George Martin, together with Ken Scott and John Smith, started the task of doing the final mixes and banding-up of *The Beatles*. They finished almost exactly 24 hours later having, in the process, used three of Abbey Road's studios simultaneously.

Chris Thomas spent several hours using an oscillator on Eric Clapton's solo on 'White My Guitar Gently Weeps' to make it sound more Beatle-esque.

16. John Lennon, with Cynthia and Brian Epstein, attended a prestigious Foyle's literary lunch held in his honour at the Dorchester Hotel on 23 April 1964. John was heavily hung over after a reception at Australia House the night before and his speech was, as a consequence, fairly short: 'Thank you all very much. God bless you.'

Several Beatle-books have managed to turn this quote into: 'Thank you very much, you have a lucky face.' In actual fact, John said *that* five days later on the *Around the Beatles* TV show.

17. On Christmas Eve 1968, a group of carol singers who turned up at Jim McCartney's home were given a rare treat. Paul, who was visiting his dad, invited them in, got out his guitar and performed 'Blackbird'. One of the singers was Neil Harrison, who would later spend over twenty years playing John in the world's premier Beatles tribute band, the Bootleg Beatles.

18. While visiting the New York apartment of Eddie Germano on 23 August 1974, John Lennon saw what he believed to be a UFO. Allegedly, as the object disappeared into the distance John was heard shouting, 'Take me with you!'

19. One of the strangest Beatles bootlegs, *Alf Together Now*, contains fragments of five – very poor quality – reel-to-reel tapes made in summer 1963 by the Beatles on a portable machine and subsequently given by John to their chauffeur, Alf Bicknell.

Highlights include home demos – 'If I Fell', an instrumental version of 'Michelle', 'Don't Bother Me' – along with sections, seemingly, recorded in Weston-super-Mare during July. These feature the Beatles (and Gerry Marsden) singing along to songs like Judy Garland's 'Over The Rainbow' on the car radio.

20. Every few years allegedly 'lost' Beatles tapes turn up – which are almost always subsequently discovered to be either not lost at all or complete hoaxes. Two recent examples deserve highlighting:

Do You Want to Know a Secret?

In July 2004, Associated Press excitedly reported that a British tourist had bought a suitcase at an Australian flea market and found in it hours of unreleased Beatles songs. It was suggested that the case may once have belonged to Mal Evans. Except it didn't. These 'unreleased recordings' turned out to be common bootleg material which had, seemingly, been compiled from a variety of sources.

Yet the story ran in newspapers and magazines around the world, with virtually no follow-up once it was debunked some weeks later. (For example, *The Times* put a snippet of a John Lennon demo – 'I'm In Love', a song he wrote for the Foremost as their follow-up to 'Hello Little Girl' – on its website so fans could hear this 'lost' classic. Had they simply done an Internet search, they would have found the song had been released on a bootleg CD over a decade earlier.)

Even more bizarre was the case of an Internet auction-site that, in December 2003, offered for sale what it claimed to be a (conveniently) erased tape of a secret Beatles reunion in November 1976. A Los Angeles studio was the alleged venue. When the owner of Davlen Sound, Len Kovner, told *Rolling Stone* that no such session had ever taken place, the website's owner claimed that Kovner was 'deathly afraid of Paul McCartney, that's why he's lying'.

WITHIN YOU, WITHOUT YOU
Outstanding influences on the Beatles' music

In addition to various 'without whom' artists (Lonnie Donegan, Eddie Cochran, Elvis, Carl Perkins) there were certain key performers who helped to shape the Beatles sound. McCartney was especially forthright on this subject during a two-hour radio show he made for the BBC at Christmas 1999.

Little Richard

The ultimate rock and roll showman, Richard Penniman emerged from Macon, Georgia in the mid-50s with a string of hysterical singles ('Tutti Frutti', 'Rip It Up', 'Lucille'). The Beatles were huge fans and performed dozens of his songs on stage.

These were mostly sung by McCartney, who had the opportunity to learn the secret of Richard's vocal technique during October and November 1962 when the Beatles and Richard appeared together at several concerts on Merseyside and in Hamburg. (Richard's organist was the 16-year-old Billy Preston.)

Two of the Beatles' finest covers were of Richard's songs: 'Long Tall Sally', and an arrangement which fused Leiber/Stoller's 'Kansas City' and his song 'Hey-Hey-Hey-Hey'. Additionally, Paul would use his Little Richard voice on many of the Beatles' wildest rock workouts ('She's A Woman', 'I'm Down', 'Birthday').

Richard remains close to Macca, often describing him as his blood brother.

Chuck Berry

Born in St Louis in 1926, Chuck Berry was the Shakespeare of R&B, writing brilliant two-minute songs with short-story lyrics full of innuendo and wordplay and a unique guitar sound. He was also a great showman, his 'duck-walk' being one of the most imitated moves in rock and roll.

Every band that emerged post-Berry (on both sides of the Atlantic) owes something to him (the Rolling Stones more than most). The Beatles were no exception, playing numerous Berry songs (several feature on *The Beatles At The Beeb*) and covering 'Roll Over Beethoven' and 'Rock And Roll Music' on record.

Buddy Holly

A prototype for every kid who stood in front of the mirror with a cricket bat as a guitar and dreamed of being a pop star. Elvis looked like he came from another planet; Buddy Holly wore glasses and looked like some bloke from the bank down the road.

Holly was a huge star in England in the late 50s – everyone who would be anyone in the subsequent beat-group movement attended gigs on Holly's 1958 UK tour. That included the Beatles. Even the group's name was, in part, a tribute to Holly's backing band, the Crickets.

Holly also wrote his own songs – clever, surprisingly sophisticated stories of teenage romance. The Beatles covered many of them in their act (the version of 'Words Of Love' on *Beatles For Sale* shows their mastery of the Crickets' sound). Perhaps more importantly, Holly showed John Lennon and Paul McCartney how to write hit singles.

The Coasters

Los Angeles-based vocal group whose performance of songs by Jerry Leiber and Mike Stoller married rock and roll, street lingo and comedy. Best known for their hits 'Yakety Yak', 'Poison Ivy' and 'Charlie Brown', the group's trademark was the bass vocals of Bobby Nunn. The Beatles were attracted to both the humour and the close harmonies of the Coasters and covered several of their songs, including 'Three Cool Cats', 'Youngblood', 'Searchin'' and 'Besame Mucho'.

The Shirelles

The archetypal girl-group, from New Jersey, the Shirelles had a huge hit in 1961 with 'Will You Still Love Me Tomorrow'. Under the direction of producer Luther Dixon, the soaring voices of Shirley Owens, Beverly Lee, Doris Kenner and Micki Harris produced magnificent close-harmony work. They were the Beatles' favourite group around the time of *Please Please Me*, reflected by respectful covers of 'Boys' and 'Baby It's You'.

Arthur Alexander

Although they only covered one of his songs on record ('Anna'), the influence of Arthur Alexander on the Beatles' songwriting is plain to see. Best known for 'A Shot Of Rhythm And Blues' (which the Beatles played live) and 'You Better Move On', the Alabama singer's lyrics were among the most intelligent and bittersweet of the era, something that Lennon, in particular, admired.

The Beatles' version of Alexander's anti-war anthem 'Soldiers Of Love (Lay Down Your Arms)', recorded for BBC radio in July 1963 (available on *The Beatles At The Beeb*), is one of their finest performances anywhere.

Bob Dylan

Contrary to common belief it was George, rather than John, who first heard Bob Dylan – he bought a copy of Dylan's extraordinary second LP *Freewheelin'* in Paris in 1964. Dylan quickly took over the Beatles' world.

Impressed by the feral maelstrom of Dylan's visionary folk songs, Lennon in particular began to experiment in a similar manner throughout 1964–65. 'I'm A Loser' and 'You've Got To Hide Your Love Away' both show the influence of Dylan's sound while 'Norwegian Wood' and 'In My Life' indicated that he'd been listening to the words too.

Dylan first met the Beatles in New York in 1964 with his friend, the journalist Al Aronowitz – famously introducing them to dope on the same day. Thereafter, Dylan remained a regular influence on the Beatles' music, particularly Harrison with whom he formed a close friendship.

The influence ran both ways as Dylan's move into electric music in 1965 seems to have been, in part, a realisation of what could be achieved by marrying his words with the music that bands like the Beatles and the Animals produced. 'The Beatles' chords were *outrageous* and their harmonies made it all valid,' Dylan would note. 'I knew they were where music had to go.'

The Beach Boys

The biggest group in America when the Beatles arrived (according to Brian Wilson, they felt very threatened by this bunch of foreigners with weird haircuts), the Beach Boys ended up as the Beatles' main international rivals for two years in the mid-60s.

Do You Want to Know a Secret?

Formed by brothers Brian, Carl and Dennis Wilson, cousin Mike Love and neighbour Al Jardine, the Beach Boys' happy, sun-bright songs about surfing, cars, girls and California made them hugely popular. However, they hid a darker, more melancholy side that began to emerge in 1964 when Brian gave up touring – after a nervous breakdown – to concentrate on recording and production.

He and McCartney, in particular, seemed to be involved in a mind-meld competition to produce the perfect pop record, something Brian came close to in 1966 with *Pet Sounds*. By that time the Beatles had already begun experimenting with Beach Boys-style harmonies ('Nowhere Man', 'Paperback Writer').

Although Wilson's dream of a 'teenage symphony to God' (*Smile*) remained unfinished for over thirty years, Paul still held Brian's work in such high regard that he managed to parody – brilliantly – the entire Beach Boys oeuvre into a three-minute slice ('Back In The USSR').

Motown

Berry Gordy's Detroit label made an astonishing impact in the early 1960s. Through writer/producers like Smokey Robinson, Holland-Dozier-Holland, and Norman Whitfield and Barrett Strong, and performers such as the Miracles, Mary Wells, the Supremes, Marvin Gaye, the Four Tops, the Isley Brothers and the Temptations, the label held a virtual stranglehold on both the British and US charts.

The Beatles used many interviews in 1963–64 to highlight their love of the Motown sound, covering three of the labels' best-known songs on *With The Beatles* ('You've Really Got A Hold On Me', 'Please Mr Postman' and 'Money') and taking Mary Wells on their British tour in October 1964.

Musically, a Motown influence regularly crops up in mid-period Beatles recordings ('Not A Second Time', 'You Won't See Me', 'Got To Get You Into My Life'). Paul has claimed that the tune for 'In My Life' was 'Miracles inspired' (there *is* a vague resemblance to 'Tracks Of My Tears').

The Animals

Newcastle's finest, the Animals' place in pop history was assured by their first two singles, which took American folk songs as covered by Bob Dylan and rearranged them with a beat-group sound. This is particularly true of 'The House Of The Rising Sun', a worldwide No. 1 in the summer of 1964.

Lennon was a close friend of the Animals' singer Eric Burdon, whom he regarded as something of a kindred spirit. Burdon would subsequently claim that he helped inspire the chorus of 'I Am The Walrus' due to some sexual fetishes, involving eggs, that Lennon had witnessed.

Musically, however, it was the Animals' keyboard sound – Alan Price's swirling Vox Continental organ – that made the biggest impression on the Beatles. The band acquired their own Vox in 1965 and the instrument featured prominently on both *Help!* and *Rubber Soul*. They even took the Vox on tour with them, giving John the opportunity to mug his way through 'I'm Down'.

The Who

It may be a coincidence, of course, but can it be that when John Lennon saw the Beatles' support band – then still called the High Numbers – at Blackpool in August 1964, he noted with interest the feedback-drenched technique of the guitarist with the enormous hooter? Eight weeks later, the Beatles were in the studio recording 'I Feel Fine' and, suddenly, the whole world knew what feedback was.

It would be a few months yet before the Who inflicted their own outrageous vision of 'Shepherd's Bush enjoyment' on the public but, when they did, by late 1965, McCartney thought enough of them to mention them in the same breath as Bob Dylan as the Beatles' biggest contemporary influences.

Sonically, the increased prominence of the bass on Beatles records around this period owes a massive debt firstly to James Jamerson and Donald 'Duck' Dunn's playing on all those classic Motown and Stax singles (respectively) but also to John Entwistle. This, despite the latter's advice to Paul not to bother with Rickenbacker basses as they were notoriously difficult to keep in tune.

Socially, the Beatles got on well with the Who, particularly with that greatest of party animals, Keith Moon, who formed friendships (especially with Ringo and John) that would last for the rest of his tragically short life.

It was, apparently, a review in *Melody Maker* of a Who single (almost certainly 1967's 'I Can See For Miles') that influenced Paul to write his own 'nastiest, dirtiest, loudest song ever', 'Helter Skelter'.

However, lest it be thought that there was total reverence in the Who camp towards the Beatles, it should be noted that when Pete Townshend appeared on the BBC2 'yoof' programme *A Whole Scene Going* in 1966 he was asked by a teenage fan whether he regarded the Beatles as 'quality'.

Townshend said that he had recently listened to a stereo Beatles LP in which the voices and the music could be isolated and that when you took away the Beatles singing, the music was 'flippin' lousy!'

Some fans still play Fantasy Bands League: since the deaths of Moon and Entwistle, Roger Daltrey and Townshend are without a rhythm section, while without the departed Lennon and Harrison, Ringo and Macca have no frontmen. Why not fuse together the two greatest bands ever into one?

This ignores one basic certainty. Any band that attempted to contain Paul and Pete would probably last about five minutes before they tried to kill each other.

The Byrds

They were, essentially, a folk/bluegrass band until they saw *A Hard Day's Night*. Dave Crosby remembers coming out of the cinema and swinging round a post, Beatles-style, in sheer joy at the opportunities presented by pop music.

In early 1965, the Byrds' recordings married the 12-string Rickenbacker guitars of the Beatles and the Searchers with the songs of Bob Dylan. 'Folk-rock' was instantly born. A mutual friendship was soon formed, particularly with Crosby and Roger McGuinn who – one summer day in LA in 1965 – introduced Ringo to acid and George to the music of Ravi Shankar.

Harrison responded by writing 'If I Needed Someone' as a direct tribute to two of his favourite Byrds songs, 'The Bells Of Rhymney' and 'She Don't Care About Time'. A distinctive Byrds influence can also be heard on *Revolver* ('Eight Miles High' could almost be a distillation of the entire LP in three-and-a-half minutes).

Donovan

A Glasgow-born folk-singer/songwriter who was dubbed 'the British Dylan' when he had his first hit, 'Catch The Wind', as an 18-year-old. Donovan Leitch subsequently had several poppy hits in the mid-60s ('Mellow Yellow', 'Sunshine Superman') with producer Mickey Most.

Donovan became friendly with the Beatles in 1966. He and his roadie Gypsy Dave lived close to McCartney in Maida Vale and would often spend the evening at Cavendish Avenue. He claims to have supplied a few uncredited lines to both 'Eleanor Rigby' and 'Yellow Submarine'.

In 1968, Donovan accompanied the Beatles to Rishikesh, and while there he introduced John and George to the finger-picking guitar style that he'd learned from his folk idols Davey Graham, Bert Janesh and John Renbourn.

As consequence, songs like 'Dear Prudence', 'Julia' and 'While My Guitar Gently Weeps' developed. George later noted that if it wasn't for Donovan, *The Beatles* would have sounded very different.

The Kinks

Classic North-London R&B band, the Kinks' early records ('You Really Got Me', 'All Day And All Of The Night') anticipated the general increase in power and volume on British singles in 1965. Around this time, the group were effectively blacklisted by the American Musicians Union and for the next three years were isolated in the UK.

This coincided with Ray Davies writing a series of beautiful vignettes of English life ('Sunny Afternoon', 'Dead End Street', 'Waterloo Sunset', 'The Village Green Preservation Society'). This brand of slightly whimsical, reflective nostalgia for a mythical England (with an element of music hall) was a big influence on 'Penny Lane' and *Sgt. Pepper's*.

THE MORE I GO INSIDE, THE MORE THERE IS TO SEE
What you can hear if you listen – very closely

Over the years, the myth has grown that every Beatles recording was a work of perfection and that any sound on it was meant to be there. Actually, given the circumstances under which they were recorded, and the primitive equipment being used, it's a miracle that there are so few mistakes and accidentally created noises on the Beatles' records.

What follows are some of the most interesting, outrageous or just plain weird sounds hidden – sometimes barely – beneath the guitars, drums and vocals, and the timings at which they can be heard. Most of these can be picked up listening to a CD with your headphones on. A word of warning, however: looking for these can seriously destroy your appreciation of the music.

'Please Please Me' (1:27)
John and Paul sing different lines simultaneously ('Why do I never ...' and 'I know you never ...' respectively). John knows he's got it wrong and his next 'Come on' begins with an audible snigger. When mixed into mono, this mistake was cleared up with a clever edit but, in stereo, the error remains.

'Twist And Shout' (2:28)
An exhilarated Paul shouts 'Hey!' as this magnificent one-take performance reaches its climax.

'I'll Get You' (1:13)
Another example of John and Paul getting confused as to which verse they're in ('I'm gonna make you mine', 'You're gonna change your mind').

'Every Little Thing' (1:27)

A clearly audible clatter is, according to legend, the sound of a music stand falling over after somebody brushed against it.

'I Feel Fine' (0:05)

Someone coughs loudly as the guitar feedback begins.

'Day Tripper' (1:50)

The worst editing mistake on any Beatles record. Listen to the guitar drop-out in the left stereo channel. Something similar happens at 2:33.

'Paperback Writer' (1:49)

Either George or John breathes heavily and then sings a single falsetto 'paperback' in the right stereo channel.

'Eleanor Rigby' (0:14)

After the word 'Eleanor', the vocals suddenly disappear from the left channel. Obviously, Geoff Emerick didn't get the fader down quickly enough.

'Tomorrow Never Knows' (1:28)

There's loud feedback from the Leslie speaker. Mind you, can *anything* going on in 'Tomorrow Never Knows' be said to have happened according to plan?

'Strawberry Fields Forever' (0:59)

The edit between the slow guitar-based version and the faster cello-and-trumpet arrangement. Legend has it that Lennon asked George Martin to perform the impossible by cutting together two takes in different tempos and keys with the memorable line 'you'll think of something!' The edit, on the word 'going' is easiest to spot by the radical change in Ringo's drumming.

At 3:27 John can be heard to shout, 'That's terrific,' while at 3:57 we get his much-quoted comment 'cranberry sauce' (*not* 'I buried Paul'). All of these are most clearly heard on the *Anthology 2* edit, along with John telling Ringo to calm down.

Do You Want to Know a Secret?

'A Day In The Life' (1:44)

Prior to the orchestral overdub, the band filled the instrumental bars with Mal Evans counting from 1 to 24. At the end of this (2:18) an alarm clock goes off and Paul can be heard counting himself into the middle section ('one' is clearly audible).

Later, at 4:51 as the final piano chord fades away, a chair can be heard creaking and someone says 'shh!' Then you get the *Sgt. Pepper's* run-out groove. And, yes, the legend *is* true – if you play it backwards, it *does* sound like, 'We'll f*ck you like a Superman.'

'All You Need Is Love' (3:13)

John shouts 'Yesterday!' shortly before he begins his amusing reprise of 'She Loves You' (3:22). Note that, in the latter, it sounds as though the lyrics are amended to 'She'd love to, yeah, yeah, yeah'.

'I Am The Walrus' (2:26)

The point at which the BBC radio version of *King Lear* first appears in the mix ('Now good sir, what are you?', 'A most poor man made tame to fortune's blows'). And after that … *you* listen to it and see what you come up with.

'Hey Bulldog' (2:52)

During the back-and-forth between John and Paul as the song fades, Paul comments, 'Don't look at me, I already have grandchildren.'

'Hey Jude' (2:58)

John, memorably, plays the wrong chord and says 'F*ckin' hell!' which is audible beneath Paul's vocal line.

'Happiness Is A Warm Gun' (0:57)

A single word ('down') from a partially erased vocal track can be heard.

'Don't Pass Me By' (1:48)

What sounds like a tray of glasses being dropped is heard in the right stereo channel.

'Helter Skelter' (3:02)

There's lots of muttering, off-mike, during this chaotic recording. The most interesting is Paul saying, 'I saw that, you little bugger!' or something very similar.

'Long Long Long' (2:31)

Described by Ian MacDonald in *Revolution in the Head* as 'the luckiest accident in any Beatles recording'. A wine bottle standing on the Leslie speaker began to rattle when Paul played a low note on the Hammond organ.

'Revolution 1' (0:02)

The spoken introduction, by Geoff Emerick, is often erroneously said to be 'Take two'. He actually says, 'I'll take it to ...' and is cut off by John's 'OK!'

'I Want You (She's So Heavy)' (4:30)

Another widely debated moment. After John's throat-shredding scream, someone (possibly Paul) can be heard giving an approving shout off-mike.

'You Never Give Me Your Money' (3:52)

John's shout of 'bloody 'ell' can be heard as the song cross-fades into 'Sun King'.

'Polythene Pam' (0:45)

The sound of a maraca being picked up is clearly audible. As the song ends and becomes 'She Came In Through The Bathroom Window', John comments, 'We'll listen to that now ... Oh, look out!'

WE ALL WANNA CHANGE THE WORLD
– The Beatles' LPs

Rubber Soul (1965)

It was recorded in just thirty days (12 October to 11 November 1965) so it could be in the shops by Christmas. Maybe it was the pressure that brought out the best in the Beatles. More likely, it was a series of new influences in their life (McCartney's interest in classical and Harrison's in Indian music, for example) plus the fact that, over the previous few months, the competition from other bands – both in Britain and America – had started to get worrying.

Whatever the reason, *Rubber Soul* was a quantum leap forward in terms of songwriting, performance and, indeed, concept. This was, as George Martin would subsequently note, 'a *fine* LP'. If nothing else it showed the Beatles' significant bouncebackability after the lethargy of *Help!*

The sessions – which also produced the 'Day Tripper'/'We Can Work It Out' single and the Booker T-influenced instrumental '12 Bar Original' – clicked almost immediately. Lennon, in particular, was on a tremendous roll, coming out of his 'Fat Elvis' period with a bunch of witty short-story songs ('Norwegian Wood', 'Nowhere Man', 'In My Life', 'Girl') which pushed McCartney to a spirited response ('Drive My Car', 'I'm Looking Through You').

George came up with his two best songs to date, 'If I Needed Someone' and 'Think For Yourself'. Even Ringo got in on the act, providing some lyrics to Lennon's 'What Goes On'.

There's a big R&B/soul influence on the LP ('The Word' is a great example) – the Beatles had, after all, spent the summer of 1965 touring the US and being exposed to Motown and Stax. (Listen, for example, to their enthusiastic parody of the Holland–Dozier–Holland sound on 'You Won't See Me'.) But there are other contemporary homages too – Dylan, the Who, the Byrds. On *Rubber Soul*, the Beatles acknowledged their friends and then pushed forward with their own agenda.

An LP to put a big smile on anyone's face (it inspired Brian Wilson to create *Pet Sounds*), *Rubber Soul* is the bracket that joins the two halves of the Beatles' career. A triumphant and stylish goodbye to the mop-top years, and a visionary prophecy of the work still to come. A 24-carat masterpiece.

WITH A LITTLE HELP FROM MY FRIENDS
Guest appearances on Beatles records

- Johnnie Scott: Flute on 'You've Got To Hide Your Love Away'.

- Tony Gilbert (violin), Sidney Sax (violin), Francisco Gabarro (cello), Kenneth Essex (viola) on 'Yesterday'. Gilbert and Sax also played in the octet on 'Eleanor Rigby' while Sax and Gabarro were part of the 40-piece orchestra that appear on 'A Day In The Life'.

- Mal Evans: A Beatle in everything but name, Mal played one-note organ on 'You Won't See Me', bass-drum on 'Yellow Submarine', harmonica on 'Being For The Benefit Of Mr Kite', sound effects (spade in gravel) on 'You Know My Name (Look Up The Number)', trumpet on 'Helter Skelter' and anvil on 'Maxwell's Silver Hammer'.

- Anil Bhagwat: Tabla on 'Love You To'.

- Eddie Thornton and Peter Coe of Georgie Fame's Blue Flames, along with session men Ian Hamer, Les Condon and Alan Branscombe provide the horn section for 'Got To Get You Into My Life'.

- Alan Civil: Contributed the stunning French horn solo on 'For No One'. Civil also played trumpet on 'Penny Lane' and 'A Day In The Life'.

- Alf Bicknell: The Beatles' chauffeur helped out with sound effects on 'Yellow Submarine' by clanking chains in a tin bath.

- Patti Harrison: George's missus not only inspired several of his best love songs, but also sang backing vocals on 'Yellow Submarine', 'All You Need Is Love' and 'Birthday'.

- Brian Jones: The Rolling Stone who died tragically young. Brian was one of the backing vocalists on 'Yellow Submarine' and also played alto-sax on 'You Know My Name (Look Up The Number)' – although it wasn't released until nine months after his death.

- Marianne Faithfull: Another celebrity friend who added backing vocals to both 'Yellow Submarine' and 'All You Need Is Love'.

- David Mason: Contributed the much-admired, Bach-influenced piccolo trumpet solo on 'Penny Lane' and also appeared on 'A Day In The Life' and 'It's All Too Much'.

- Marijke Koger: Artist and Fool member, he played tambourine on 'A Day In The Life'.

- Members of Sounds Incorporated: Shared many tours with the Beatles during the mid-60s and supplied the brass section on 'Good Morning, Good Morning'.

- Neil Aspinall: Roadie and key associate, he played harmonica on 'Being For The Benefit Of Mr Kite', tambura on 'Within You Without You' and percussion on 'Magical Mystery Tour'.

- Mick Jagger: Although the rumour that he sang backing vocals on 'Baby, You're A Rich Man' remains unconfirmed, Mick definitely appears on the massed chorus of 'All You Need Is Love'. Among the other friends and musicians who attended the *Our World* broadcast/recording of 'All You Need Is Love' and appeared bellowing along on the chorus were Keith Richards, Keith Moon, Jane Asher, Mike McCartney, Graham Nash, Gary Leeds and Hunter Davies.

- Jack Emblow: Played the accordion on 'All You Need Is Love'.

- The Mike Sammes Singers: Sang the memorable 'Oompah, oompah, stick it up yer jumper' finale to 'I Am The Walrus' and also appeared on 'Good Night'.

- Ashish Khan: Provided the unique Arabesque sarod on 'The Inner Light'.

- Ronnie Scott: Jazz saxophonist and London club-owner, played the rasping sax solo on 'Lady Madonna'.

- Lizzie Bravo and Gaylene Pease: Two of the self-styled Apple Scruffs (who camped outside Abbey Road and Savile Row in all weathers). Invited into the studio by Paul, they provided backing vocals on 'Across The Universe'.

- Don Lang: A singer in the early 60s ('The Witch Doctor'), Lang played trombone on 'Revolution'.

Jack Fallon: Played the fiddle solo on 'Don't Pass Me By'.

Jimmy Scott: Nigerian percussionist and friend of McCartney who, according to legend, invented the phrase 'Ob-La-Di, Ob-La-Da'. He played on the first, lighter, version of the song (see *Anthology 3*) although not on the initially released version. Jimmy subsequently recorded with the Rolling Stones.

Nicky Hopkins: The only man to feature on records by the Who, the Rolling Stones *and* the Beatles. A celebrated session pianist, Nicky appears on 'Revolution'.

Eric Clapton: Invited along by his mate George Harrison to provide the solo for 'While My Guitar Gently Weeps', Clapton's identity was obscured in contemporary publicity with the claim that the guitarist involved had actually been 'Eddie Clayton'.

Jackie Lomax: Former member of the Liverpool R&B band the Undertakers, Jackie was George Harrison's protégé in the early days at Apple. He sang backing vocals on 'Dear Prudence'.

Yoko Ono: Provided backing vocals on 'Birthday' and a solitary solo vocal line to 'The Continuing Story Of Bungalow Bill' as well as collaborating with John and George on 'Revolution 9' and 'What's the New Mary Jane?'

Billy Preston: Organ on 'I've Got A Feeling', 'Get Back', 'Don't Let Me Down', 'Let It Be', 'One After 909', 'I Want You (She's So Heavy)' and 'Something'.

Jeff Lynne: Backing vocals and guitar on 'Real Love'.

THINK FOR YOURSELF
George Harrison – Scouser of distinction

Irony figures strongly in George Harrison's story. People couldn't get a handle on him in the 60s, unlike his more two-dimensional colleagues, so he became 'the quiet one'. He was also, it was said, the Beatle most obsessed with money and, later, the one who went all religious and weird.

John might have been 'the funny one' but which Beatle ended up working with the *Monty Python* lads? Paul wrote most of the great ballads, but who penned 'Something', which Frank Sinatra described as 'the greatest love song of the last fifty years'?

When he died in 2001, many of the world's newspapers were filled with cartoons that depicted George joining John in heaven, full of overt Christian imagery. The irony of this would not have been lost on one of the world's best-known Buddhists.

George could be stubborn and difficult – something occasionally reflected in both his music and his lyrics. He was probably the first Beatle for whom the merry-go-round stopped being fun. Lennon died shortly after stating that he felt betrayed at having been virtually ignored in George's autobiography. And it was only at the very end of his life that George and Paul got to grips with their sometimes fractious relationship.

The product of a close-knit family, of all the Beatles George probably had the keenest sense of traditional Northern working-class values – keep your feet on the ground and remember who your *real* friends are. He valued privacy and loyalty, and was also a man of great humour who loved motor racing and James Bond films.

George, as has been noted, served a similar role in the Beatles to Dave Davies in the Kinks – a keen collector of musical ideas to be put into a collective pot. He brought his bandmates' attention to artists as diverse as Bob Dylan, Otis Redding and Ravi Shankar.

There must have been days when he wished he was in another band, however, particularly days when he had to do ten John and Paul songs before they'd get to one of his. That's one of the main reasons why *All Things Must Pass* is such a wonderful LP; because he had four years' worth of accumulated classics ready to go on the day the Beatles broke up.

George got total respect when he was hanging out with Clapton and Dylan but there were times when he got precious little in his own band. 'The main fault with John and Paul,' he noted in 1987, '[was] they were so busy *being* John and Paul, they failed to notice who else was around at the time.'

In later years George became the Beatle who looked back on the madness with the least affection but, often, the most clarity. The description of him as 'a dry sod' is spot-on. His contributions to *Anthology* were much more pithy than Paul and Ringo's occasionally rose-tinted memories, yet he was seldom cynical with it and he was always proud of the music.

Nevertheless, George would note that he actually preferred his friend Eric Idle's 1978 spoof *The Rutles* (in which Harrison himself appeared). 'It liberated me from being a Beatle,' he said. Perhaps it was the trousers.

His success with *The Concert for Bangladesh* and, subsequently, HandMade Films never stopped him being 'Beatle George', something that he clearly resented. But George Harrison didn't allow that energy to become consumed by negativity.

And, though his view of Beatles fans sometimes appeared to hover between bemusement and outright hostility, he could be the tenderest of them all when the mood took him. ('Apple Scruffs' is one of the most perceptive songs about fandom ever written, and can melt the hardest heart to slush.)

When asked in 1999 about the reissue of *Yellow Submarine* on DVD George philosophically noted, 'In my heart, I still am on that mountain in India somewhere – and that suits me.'

WE ALL WANNA CHANGE THE WORLD
– The Beatles' LPs

Revolver (1966)

Having had their first decent (three-month) holiday since 1962, the Beatles arrived at Abbey Road refreshed and inspired. Their influences were now not just musical, they were chemical too. Recorded between 6 April and 21 June 1966, *Revolver* was the epitome of the Beatles' acid period. Not only was LSD a notable influence on the sound ('I'm Only Sleeping', 'Tomorrow Never Knows'), it was all over the concept as well.

Amid Lennon's outrageous evocations of expanded universal conscious-ness ('Tomorrow Never Knows', 'She Said She Said') and Harrison's first foray into his Hindi phase ('Love You To'), McCartney – still a pot man through-and-through – was letting his imagination trip on baroque musical dreamscapes to quite devastating effect.

'Eleanor Rigby', 'Here, There And Everywhere', 'For No One', 'Got To Get You Into My Life' – mature, sophisticated tone poems in the tradition of Cole Porter and Leonard Bernstein – easily defeat Philip Norman's igno-rant assertion that John Lennon was three-quarters of the Beatles. The case for the defence, frankly, rests on *Revolver* alone.

Revolver – like its companion-piece single, 'Paperback Writer'/'Rain' – is effortlessly inventive, full of great songs: 'And Your Bird Can Sing', 'Taxman', 'Good Day Sunshine'. And, if one accepts 'Yellow Submarine' for what it is, no fillers.

George, in *Anthology*, described *Rubber Soul* and *Revolver* as like part one and part two of the same record, but even in a few short months the Beatles had developed and, in the process, made quite possibly the most influential record of all time.

THINGS WE SAID TODAY
Quotes (part 2)

● John, asked if success had spoiled the Beatles: 'You don't see us running out and buying bowler hats, do you? I think we've pretty well succeeded in remaining ourselves.'

● Ringo, on whether the atom bomb or dandruff was the bigger threat to the Beatles enduring popularity: 'Bombs. We've already got dandruff.'

● Paul, describing the worst part of success: 'It's like a girl, isn't it? It's only when you've caught up with her and looked back that you find the best bit was the chase.'

● John, it having been suggested that most Beatles fans thought of them as decent, clean-living chaps: 'It's just an image, and it's the wrong one. Look at the Rolling Stones. Rough as guts. We did that first and now they've pinched it.'

● George lives up to his image as the quiet one: 'I like parties and a bit of fun like everyone else, but there's nothing better than a bit of peace and quiet. Sitting around a big fire with your slippers on and watching the telly, that's the life.'

● John, when asked what he thought the Beatles' music did for the kids: 'If we knew, we'd form another group and be managers.'

● George's reported reaction when the Beatles' Lockheed Electra jet had to make an emergency landing in Portland with one of the engines on fire: 'This should stop [the press] asking how much longer we're gonna last.'

● A reporter asks about the meaning of the group's name. 'It's just a name, like shoe,' replies John. 'See, we could have been called the Shoes,' continues Paul.

● John, asked if Merseybeat had changed: 'There's no such thing, it's something the press made up. It's rock and roll, it just so happens we write it.'

● Ringo, on what he would do if the fans ever made it past the police: 'Die laughing.'

TAKE THIS BROTHER, MAY IT SERVE YOU WELL!
Revolution 9 – a defence!

When *The Beatles* appeared, most of the million people – according to the *Guinness Book of Records* – who bought copies on the day of release reached side four and, when they listened to the second-to-last track, assumed that they'd bought a faulty record.

What, you mean it's *supposed* to sound like that?

Opinion quickly divided into two camps and, pretty much, that's still the situation with regard to 'Revolution 9' – the oddest thing the Beatles ever recorded. There's no such thing as a neutral option: you either love it (a few people do) or you *hate* it and everything it stands for (that would be everyone else on planet Earth).

'Revolution 9' was a John Lennon-produced sound-collage, an example of avant-garde sonic experimentation that, actually, wasn't a million miles removed from some of the Beatles' previous ventures. After all, 'Tomorrow Never Knows' had tape-loops too. Admittedly, it also had *a tune*.

This form – *musique concrète* – wasn't new either; John Cage and Karlheinz Stockhausen had been composing such left-field modernist pieces for twenty years. The difference, of course, was that *The Beatles* was a mainstream pop record, bought by millions of people who'd never heard *Imaginary Landscapes* or *Gruppen*.

Probably the biggest influence on Lennon's decision to make 'Revolution 9' was Yoko Ono, who appears on it with her sensual exhortation to listeners to 'become naked'.

Having compiled the collage over several weeks – initially as part of an extended piece that included 'Revolution 1' – John put it together on 20 June 1968, mixing in backward tapes, orchestral surges, fragments of studio chatter and various sound effects.

Then, along with George and Yoko, he recorded hours of prose, poetry and vocal nonsense which were mixed in and out of the finished piece to give the impression of half-heard whispers, a badly tuned radio or voices from the beyond.

'Revolution 9' is a truly sinister piece of work (Harrison, a year later, noted that he'd only played it once and that it had freaked him out). It's disturbing to listen to – Lennon said that he'd wanted to capture 'the sound of a revolution'. Actually, it's a much less literal experience than that.

As some critics have noted, the final three tracks on The Beatles – 'Cry Baby Cry', 'Revolution 9' and 'Good Night' – provide a very interesting psychological profile of their author. A chilling little nursery rhyme, the sound of a nightmare and a nostalgic lullaby.

There's a distinct element of childhood in the mood and texture of 'Revolution 9', something that the McCartney song-fragment ('Can you take me back where I've been') that prefigures the piece greatly enhances.

Paul, reportedly, hated 'Revolution 9' and tried everything he could to get it removed from the LP, although he's never publicly talked about it – it's a significant omission from Many Years From Now, for example. Speculation now exists that Paul's main complaint wasn't so much concerning the track itself (which, as noted, wasn't that different from some of the things he'd been doing himself) as the fact that he hadn't been asked to participate.

'Revolution 9' remains the least-played eight minutes in the Beatles discography.

SHE'S LEAVING HOME
Studios the Beatles worked in other than
Abbey Road

From the moment they first walked into the EMI studios in St John's Wood in June 1962, the Beatles would remain associated with the place for the rest of their career.

They could, occasionally, get frustrated at the conservatism, EMI bureaucracy and the limitations of the four-track machines they recorded their best work on. They would, sometimes, hatch elaborate plans to record elsewhere (*Revolver* in Nashville, for instance). But, for one reason or another, it never happened. Abbey Road was home.

However, on a few isolated occasions, the Beatles did venture further afield:

EMI Pathé Marconi Studio, Paris

The Beatles were reluctant visitors to EMI's Paris studio on 29 January 1964 to record German-language versions of 'She Loves You' and 'I Want To Hold Your Hand' ('Sie Liebt Dich' and 'Komm Gib Mir Deine Hand' respectively). However, having got that chore out of the way, they used some studio-time to record a new song, 'Can't Buy Me Love', in four takes.

Regent Sound Studios

Unable to get into Abbey Road on 9 February 1967, George Martin booked the Beatles into this studio on Tottenham Court Road to record 'Fixing A Hole'. Regent Sound was where much of the Rolling Stones' mid-60s work was recorded.

Olympic Sound Studio

Situated in Barnes, South London, Olympic was probably England's top independent studio during the late 60s; the Stones recorded *Beggars Banquet* and *Let*

It Bleed there, for example. The Beatles first used Olympic in 1967, recording 'Baby, You're A Rich Man' and the backing track for 'All You Need Is Love'. (Eddie Kramer, who engineered these sessions, is best known for his groundbreaking work with Jimi Hendrix.)

The band returned to Olympic in March 1969 to mix the January *Get Back* session with Glyn Johns. They would subsequently record 'You Never Give Me Your Money' and overdubs for 'Something' in May.

De Lane Lea Studio

Near Holburn tube station, the Who would cut material for their *The Who Sell Out* LP at De Lane Lea shortly after the Beatles recorded 'It's All Too Much' there in May 1967.

Chappell Studios

A small independent studio on Maddox Street (just off Regent Street), the Beatles recorded 'Your Mother Should Know' at Chappell in August 1967.

Trident Studios

In the heart of Soho, on Wardour Street, Trident would subsequently become the studio where David Bowie recorded *Hunky Dory* and *Ziggy Stardust*. Both Paul and George used Trident in the summer of 1968, producing recordings by Mary Hopkin and Jackie Lomax respectively. The Beatles were probably most attracted to Trident because it had eight-track facilities.

'Hey Jude', 'Dear Prudence', 'Honey Pie', 'Savoy Truffle' and 'Martha My Dear' were cut at Trident between August and October 1968, and the Beatles returned there in February the following year to record 'I Want You (She's So Heavy)'.

Apple Studios

Magic Alex had promised to design the Beatles a state-of-the-art 72-track studio in the basement of Savile Row. In the event, his plans proved unworkable and the Beatles ended up recording what would become the *Let It Be* LP in Apple on equipment borrowed from Abbey Road.

WE ALL WANNA CHANGE THE WORLD
– The Beatles' LPs

Sgt. Pepper's Lonely Hearts Club Band (1967)

Begun on 24 November 1966 and completed on 20 April 1967, the *Sgt. Pepper's* sessions have become so legendary (and so hyped) that it's difficult to be objective about the music that emerged from them. In that time, the Beatles recorded what was probably the best double-sided single ever made ('Strawberry Fields Forever'/'Penny Lane') and this much-loved LP (together with the out-take 'Only A Northern Song' and the still-unreleased 'Carnival Of Light').

These were clearly extraordinary sessions (they don't come much more extraordinary than the several that produced 'A Day In The Life') and with the help of George Martin and Geoff Emerick's stunning production, the idea that *Sgt. Pepper's* was some kind of concept LP became a fashionable one. But, it isn't.

The LP's release was regarded as a major event in world terms and, almost immediately, the music industry collectively decided that *Sgt. Pepper's* was the greatest thing since sliced bread. It wasn't.

It *was* a good LP for its time, that much remains obvious. The songs – Lennon's twin Lewis Carrollathons 'Lucy In The Sky With Diamonds' and 'Being For The Benefit Of Mr Kite', McCartney's 'She's Leaving Home', 'Fixing A Hole' and 'Lovely Rita', Harrison's gorgeous 'Within You Without You' – are mostly terrific.

But *Sgt. Pepper's* was as much a media event as an LP of classic rock and roll (the deliberate lavishness of the cover, the release in a burst of publicity, managing to get themselves banned by the BBC for alleged drug allusions) and it suffers *as* an LP of classic rock and roll for exactly that reason.

The Beatles themselves regarded it as an important statement, but within days they were on to their next project. To ascribe to *Sgt. Pepper's* some of the things that (very serious-minded) people have over the years is to believe that, frankly, the world stopped turning on 1 June 1967 when the LP was released. It didn't.

Still, having said all that, listen to 'A Day In The Life' in the dark with a candle burning and you'll be inches away from a quasi-religious experience. You can cut any band which manages *that* a lot of slack.

STANDING ON THE CAST-IRON SHORE
Surrealism in Beatles lyrics

As early as 1965, John Lennon was aware that the Beatles were developing an audience among the 'intelligentsia' who seemed intent on finding hidden meanings in the band's lyrics. (During the recording of 'You've Got To Hide Your Love Away', on one take John mistakenly sang 'two foot small' rather than 'tall' and suggested leaving it in as 'the pseuds'll love it!')

Nevertheless, most of John's wordplay at this stage tended to be confined to his books, and it was Paul who first began to dabble in surrealistic lyrical imagery; witness Eleanor Rigby, keeping her face in a jar by the door, or the cascade of characters living under Penny Lane's shimmering, hallucinogenic blue suburban skies (where, if you notice, it's raining and sunny at the same time).

By *Sgt. Pepper's*, it was open season: inspired by Bob Dylan getting away with increasingly obscure (and obtuse) lyrics, Lennon decided *he* wanted in on the action. Hence 'Lucy In The Sky With Diamonds' marrying a Lewis Carroll-style fantasy setting with *Goon Show* nonsense language. (Plasticine porters with looking-glass ties is pure Spike Milligan.) And, as for 'I Am The Walrus' … Enough said.

The *Yellow Submarine* movie beautifully took the Beatles' psychedelic-phase lyrics and contextualised them in a visual world of the subconscious, full of Blue Meanies and Kinky-Boot Beasts. But, even as the band were slipping quietly out of the back door to Pepperland, they were still writing songs like 'Lady Madonna', 'Happiness Is A Warm Gun' and 'Cry Baby Cry' with their elaborate metaphors, iconic characters (the man with multicoloured mirrors on his hobnail boots) and sinister wordplay.

They knew the fans were rabidly seeking such references and even sent the whole thing up in 'Glass Onion', a gloriously over-the-top 'make sense of *this*' challenge that most listeners failed to appreciate the irony of.

Abbey Road features some outrageous lyrical conceits ('Come Together' most notably) but by the end of their career the Beatles were crash-landing back to Earth in common with many of their contemporaries.

The 1960s were almost over, the drugs were – depending on your point of reference – either just wearing off or just starting to take effect and realism, allegory and *realpolitik* seemed to be the way forward.

Certainly, the Beatles' 1969 lyrics – for all their witty allusions to cross-dressing ('Get Back'), gobbledygook ('Dig a Pony') and drug-fuelled paranoia ('She Came in Through the Bathroom Window') – suggested a group of men in their late 20s realising it was time to get their shit together.

THE INNER LIGHT
Unreleased Beatles performances

For years after they split up, legends were whispered among Beatles fans about the unheard gems lurking in EMI's vaults. Titles were discussed – 'Peace Of Mind', 'Pink Litmus Paper Shirt', 'Colliding Circles', 'India'. The record company always denied most of this, stating that there were only a handful of unreleased Beatles recordings and that they were unreleased for a very good reason. They were crap.

In the 1980s EMI almost put out an LP called *Sessions* featuring a handful of these recordings and alternate takes of previously well-known songs, but the Beatles blocked its release. With an avalanche of releases in the 1990s (the two-CD *Beatles At The Beeb* and the six-CD *Anthology* project) surely there couldn't be anything remotely worth listening to left? George Martin said as much when asked that very question.

Nevertheless, there are, indeed, unreleased Beatles performances. Whether they *should* be released is a different matter but, in the spirit of the fan within all of us, here's an imaginary twenty-song CD called, for the sake of argument, *The Sound Of Beatle-Barrels Being Scraped*.

'Love Of The Loved' – 'Take Good Care Of My Baby' – 'To Know Her Is To Love Her'

Tapes of the Beatles' Decca audition, on 1 January 1962, began circulating on bootlegs in the mid-70s. Eventually an LP (called *The Silver Beatles*) was released, the legality of which is certainly open to question. This contained some of these recordings but, significantly, omitted the three Lennon/McCartney originals. A smattering of the Decca songs also appear on *Anthology 1*.

'Love Of The Loved', for some reason, has never been released anywhere. It's a slightly mannered performance by McCartney but it's interesting to listen to and the song itself (which the author subsequently gave to Cilla Black for her first single) is certainly no worse than 'Like Dreamers Do'.

George Harrison warbling his way through Bobby Vee's contemporary hit 'Take Good Care Of My Baby' shows how the Beatles might have sounded if George Martin hadn't got his hands on them. Phil Spector's 'To Know Her Is To Love Her' (the song through which John, Paul and George learned to sing three-part harmonies) is definitely worthy of a place in any Beatles collection.

'Dream Baby' – 'A Picture Of You' – 'Some Other Guy' – 'Beautiful Dreamer'

Although the Beatles radio recordings are well covered in *The Beatles At The Beeb* (1994), a few gems escaped – mainly due to the poor quality of the off-air recordings.

Roy Orbison's 'Dream Baby', sung by Paul, was the first Beatles performance ever broadcast (on *Teenager's Turn* in March 1962). George's worthwhile stab at Joe Brown's 'A Picture Of You' comes from three months later. (Brown would subsequently become one of Harrison's best friends.)

'Some Other Guy' was a vital part of the Beatles' act circa 1962–63. It, and the rather hammy beat-arrangement of Stephen Foster's standard 'Beautiful Dreamer' (another song the Beatles played live during the Helen Shapiro tour), were performed on their first appearance on *Saturday Club* in January 1963.

'Red Hot'

During the final days of 1962, the Beatles were stuck in Hamburg playing a two-week residency at the Star Club. On a number of these dates (probably four in total, including their show on New Year's Eve) Adrian Barber, the club's stage manager, recorded on a portable four-track Philips machine the Beatles sets, along with those of a number of other bands playing at the club.

These tapes were given to Ted 'Kingsize' Taylor, leader of another of the groups recorded, the Dominoes. Many years later, Taylor made an agreement with Allan Williams and Bill Harry to get the live recordings released and, in 1977, a 26-song representative sample, *The Beatles Live! At The Star Club, Hamburg*, appeared on the Lingasong label. And it's fantastic stuff, despite the dubious sound quality.

Over the following years many variations on these recordings emerged, sometimes adding the odd song or two that hadn't previously been released. That is, until 1998 when Apple finally mounted a successful challenge to the legality of the tape's ownership.

One song, however, remains unreleased – except for a short snatch of it being used on the soundtrack of *Anthology* – a stinging version of John singing Ronnie Hawkins' 'Red Hot'.

'Carnival Of Light'

A thirteen-minute-plus 'freak out' of random sound effects and vocal interjections recorded on 5 January 1967. Paul had been asked by his friend David Vaughan if the Beatles could provide some music to be played at a 'happening' that Vaughan and his partners were planning for the Roundhouse later in the month.

Until it was revealed by Mark Lewisohn in the 80s, no one even knew 'Carnival Of Light' existed. Because very few people have even *heard* it, the recording has acquired the kind of 'suppressed masterpiece' reputation that 'What's The New Mary Jane?' used to have.

McCartney reportedly wanted to include it (or a fragment of it) on *Anthology* but the idea was scuppered by Harrison. It remains to be seen whether it will ever see the light of day.

'Sour Milk Sea' – 'Circles' – 'Child Of Nature'

One day in late May 1968, just before going into the studios to start *The Beatles*, the band convened at George's house to tape reference-purposes demos of the dozens of songs they'd written in India.

Some years later, a tape of the recordings emerged and became the source of one of the great Beatles bootlegs, *The Black Album*. Several of the performances were finally given an official release on *Anthology 3*.

Curiously, two George Harrison songs, 'Sour Milk Sea' and 'Circles', were left unreleased. The former Harrison gave to Jackie Lomax; it was one of the first singles released on Apple in August 1968. The latter, a rather monotone song about karma, would eventually be recorded by George fourteen years later on *Gone Troppo*.

Lennon's 'Child Of Nature' (sometimes called 'On The Road To Rishikesh') is a fascinating song, written while the singer was still under the influence of the Maharishi. It obviously had some sentimental value to Lennon – not only did he try it out again during the *Let It Be* rehearsals, but he would eventually use the tune (with different lyrics) for his 1971 solo classic 'Jealous Guy'.

'Goodbye'

A lovely McCartney song, written specifically for Apple's Mary Hopkin (Paul produced her recording of the song on 1 March 1969 at Morgan Studios in Willesden). A demo by Paul – probably recorded in December 1968 – has long circulated on bootlegs.

'Honey Hush' – 'Suzy's Parlour' – 'Commonwealth'/'Get Off' – 'Madman' – 'Watching Rainbows' – 'I Lost My Little Girl' – 'Dig It'

The *Get Back/Let It Be* rehearsals/sessions from January 1969 are the source of most Beatles bootlegs and many myths. Virtually every second of the group's activities, musical or otherwise, during the month was taped.

The rehearsals, at Twickenham, are often full of unlistenable garbage, but every so often a little gem will emerge from hours of tedious repetition and farting about. An energetic cover version of Big Joe Turner's 'Honey Hush' from 9 January is a classic example, more than justifying Glyn Johns' assertion that, actually, the sessions weren't nearly as black as they would be subsequently painted by John and George.

'Suzy's Parlour' (often called 'Suzy Parker') is a brilliant piece of Lennon nonsense with very euphemistic lyrics ('when you get to Suzy's parlour, everybody gets well done!') that actually ended up in the *Let It Be* movie.

A controversial inclusion in any release would be the ten-minute combination of a couple of pieces of social commentary, also from 9 January. As most fans will know, 'Get Back' began as an anti-racist parody of racist views about Pakistanis 'living in a council flat'. That subsequently changed (since most fascist numbskulls seem to think that irony is something their mum does with their shirts) but this train of thought seemed to have tickled McCartney's fancy.

'Commonwealth' is a rollicking three-minute slab of make-it-up-as-we-go-along rock and roll concerning the Tory politician Enoch Powell, whose comments the previous year in his 'rivers of blood' speech had done much to create racial tension in Britain. The lyrics are improvised and sometimes Macca loses his thread, but it's really funny. Especially interesting is the point where Paul makes a joke ('I'd join the Commonwealth but it's much too wealthy for me') and John chips in and improves it ('too *common* for me!')

As the song staggers to a close, George starts to lead the Beatles into 'For You Blue' but Lennon and McCartney are having too much fun and start on a seven-minute-plus blues vamp usually described as either 'Get Off!' or 'White Power'. This develops into a revealing litany of call-and-response with names of friends, colleagues and contemporary musicians being invoked. It's brilliant and, again, ends on a terrific Lennon joke concerning the name of the Incredible String Band.

Two Lennon fragments tried out at Twickenham, 'Madman' and 'Watching Rainbows' are, basically, variations on the same song (both vaguely inspired by Dylan's 'Quinn the Eskimo', which the Beatles also messed about with during these rehearsals). The former was worked for several days (and was also, briefly, revived in the studio at Apple), but the latter was only attempted once – on 14 January.

Although the Beatles became a touch more disciplined when they got into Apple Studios to begin recording Let It Be, they still regularly slipped into improvisations and this is best exemplified by the version of McCartney's 'I Lost My Little Girl' (the first song he ever wrote) that the Beatles jammed on 24 January. Surprisingly, it's Lennon singing it and he seems to be having great fun making up new lyrics.

The theme of improvisation reached its peak on 26 January with 'Dig It', part of which was featured in the Let It Be movie. It is another we-just-made-this-up free-for-all (twelve minutes of it in total) featuring McCartney's stepdaughter Heather wailing à la Yoko in the background with vocals from Paul, George and John. Thirty seconds of 'Dig It' featured on the Let It Be LP; much more is required.

ACT NATURALLY
The Beatles' movies

In the early 60s, any pop star who'd had half-a-dozen hits would be offered a movie. Not just Elvis, but Cliff, Tommy Steele, Adam Faith and Billy Fury – they *all* made films. It was a natural way to expand a career into being an 'all-round entertainer' in the frank expectation that this pop-malarkey was not going to last forever.

The Beatles were no exception. As early as summer 1963, they were offered a cameo in Robert Hartford-Davies's *The Yellow Teddy Bears*. They turned it down, allegedly because they were required to perform songs written by someone else. (In addition, it's hard to see Brian Epstein allowing the Beatles to feature in a movie that concerned a clique in an exclusive girls' school who wear the eponymous bears to signify they'd lost their virginity.)

But it was just postponing the inevitable; here is a catalogue of the Beatles on film.

The First US Visit (1964)

When the Beatles flew to New York in February 1964 they were accompanied by cinéma vérité filmmakers Albert and David Maysels. Some of the brothers' footage was subsequently licensed to Granada for a TV documentary, *Yeah! Yeah! Yeah! The Beatles in New York*. The rest was intended for a movie.

The Maysels film – *What's Happening?* – captured perfectly that amazing fortnight; the press conferences, *The Ed Sullivan Show* appearances, hanging out with Murray the K and the Ronettes at the Peppermint Lounge, the train to Washington, fun-in-the-sun in Miami. It was hardly seen for many years, not least due to the fact that parts of it mirrored *A Hard Day's Night* uncomfortably.

The Maysels went on to make one of the great rock documentaries, *Gimme Shelter* with the Rolling Stones. Finally, Apple acquired the rights to *What's Happening?* and it was released – as *The First US Visit* – on DVD in 2003 complete with numerous deleted scenes.

A Hard Day's Night (1964)

CLANG! *That* chord (G-11th suspended 4th) and we're off. The Beatles are running for their lives down Boston Place towards Marylebone Station and into cinema history. It's been said before, but it bears repeating, *A Hard Day's Night* isn't just an evocation of Beatlemania, it *is* Beatlemania.

The film was only made because United Artists discovered a loophole in the Beatles' deal with Capitol that didn't cover movie soundtracks. The company's thinking was that even if the film was a flop, they could recover their costs in record sales.

The chosen scriptwriter was Alun Owen, a TV dramatist (McCartney had particularly admired his 1959 kitchen-sink teleplay *No Trams to Lime Street*). Owen accompanied the Beatles for a few days in November 1963 and quickly picked up their personality traits. Lennon would later accuse Owen of being 'a professional Liverpudlian' to which Owen memorably replied, 'It's better than being an amateur one!'

Owen's script was sharp, pacey and witty (and helped get the Scouse slang expression 'grotty' into the dictionary). It followed two days in the Beatles' lives and was, as Ringo memorably noted, 'a train and a room and a car and a room and a room and a room'.

Wilfred Brambell, Britain's favourite dirty old man in the sitcom *Steptoe and Son*, played Paul's 'clean' grandfather while Norman Rossington and John Junkin were cast as Neil and Mal substitutes Norm and Shake. (Interestingly, there's no Brian Epstein figure in the movie.) The rest of the cast was made up of reliable character actors (Richard Vernon, Frank Thornton, Victor Spinetti, Kenneth Haigh, etc.).

Ringo got most plaudits for his scene with the teenage David Janson and John had a fine solo spot – an amusing exchange with Anna Quayle. George was the unexpected bonus, casually throwing off atom bombs of wit from the sidelines ('filled his head with notions, seemingly'). He also met his future wife, Patti Boyd, on-set (she plays one of the schoolgirls on the train).

Ironically, it was Paul – the 'theatrical' Beatle who was living with an actress – who seemed the most self-conscious. His big solo scene (with Isla Blair) was cut after filming.

A Hard Day's Night was made ludicrously quickly by Dick Lester and his crew – just seven weeks' principal filming in March and April 1964. It had to be. United

Artists (fearing the Beatles' popularity might crumble at any moment) needed it in cinemas by July.

In the event, the film was a huge hit, memorably described by Andrew Sallis in *Village Voice* as 'the *Citizen Kane* of jukebox movies'. Flattering as that description is, it actually undersells *A Hard Day's Night*'s achievements. *Citizen Kane* is merely a very great movie. *A Hard Day's Night* is part of a socio-political revolution.

For many, *A Hard Day's Night* remains the truest celluloid portrait of the Beatles and, in the 'Can't Buy Me Love' sequence, *the* perfect evocation of an era. At the end of three minutes of joyous abandon, an angry representative of authority arrives to put an end to all this frivolity. 'Sorry we hurt your field, Mister,' says George with resignation. At the end of the day, it was still *their* world. But it wouldn't be for much longer.

Help!

The Beatles' second film divides opinion. Many, including at least one of the group, felt it was a letdown after *A Hard Day's Night*, that the band were reduced to being 'extras in our own movie'. The alternative viewpoint is that *Help!* is the fantasy mirror image to *A Hard Day's Night*'s realism. The Swingin' Sixties that everybody imagines happened rather than the real one.

The initial script – by American Marc Behn – was extensively rewritten by Charles Wood and shooting got under way in February 1965 in the Bahamas (other location filming took place in Austria). This time the cast included Leo McKern, Eleanor Bron, Victor Spinetti, Roy Kinnear and Patrick Cargill, with cameos from the likes of Warren Mitchell, Dandy Nichols and Alfie Bass. A sequence was shot featuring Frankie Howerd but it ended up on the cutting-room floor.

The plot was madcap run-around nonsense involving an Eastern religious cult who want to murder Ringo. It's been described – by PC thugs – as racist, which is a little like saying *A Hard Day's Night* is sexist because there aren't many female characters. In actual fact, *Help!* was hugely influential, not only on obvious things like *The Monkees*. *Help!* encapsulates a fantasy 60s London in the same way that *The Avengers* or *The Italian Job* do.

There are many great moments – the 'fiendish thingy', Paul's Exciting Adventure on the Floor, the tiger – and, despite the overwhelming impression that John,

Paul, George and Ringo are floating through the entire movie on a marijuana high ('boys, are you buzzing?'), plenty of laughs too.

Help! remains massively (and snobbishly) underrated and is long overdue a DVD release which, hopefully, its fortieth anniversary in 2005 will see.

The Magical Mystery Tour (1967)

It was all Paul's fault! The idea of making their own film seemed quite possible to the Beatles in the 'anything can be done' atmosphere of the immediate post-*Sgt. Pepper's* period. So they set about plotting (after a fashion) and directing a 60-minute movie that they then sold to the BBC for transmission on Boxing Day. Big mistake.

The Magical Mystery Tour is a mess, frankly. Some of it is quite funny, but it needed a good editor for it to work. A script would've helped, too. Individual scenes are interesting (Jessie's dream, for example) and the musical sequences are, mostly, great. But many of the cast – including cult poet Ivor Cutler – look as though they haven't a clue what's going on around them. Victor Spinetti appears in his third Beatle-related project.

Slaughtered by most of the critics (the *Guardian*'s Keith Dewhurst was a notable exception, describing it as 'an inspired freewheeling achievement'), *The Magical Mystery Tour* was the first crack in the public perception that the Beatles were infallible.

Still, when all's said and done, and as McCartney is proud to note, there aren't many places where you can see John Lennon performing 'I Am The Walrus' backed by a troupe of dancing policemen.

Yellow Submarine (1968)

It began as a contractual obligation, a project that the Beatles wanted little to do with. Al Brodax's company, King Features, had produced a Beatles cartoon TV series (which the Beatles hated) and proposed a full-length animated feature. The group agreed purely to fulfil their three-movie contract with United Artists.

Director George Dunning and his team started work in August 1967. The key appointment was designer Heinz Edelmann, who devised the film's unique pop-art-verging-on-psychedelia look. The story was by Lee Mintoff although much of the final script was by Erich Segal, who later wrote *Love Story*. At George

Harrison's insistence, the Scaffold's Roger McGough provided some (uncredited) rewrites to ensure that the dialogue was reasonably authentic (and funny).

The reluctant Beatles gradually warmed to the project. (How could anybody not love a film that opens with the line: 'Once upon a time ... or maybe twice'?) They provided four new songs for the soundtrack and even filmed a brief appearance at the end to warn audiences that Blue Meanies had been sighted in the vicinity of their theatre.

Circumstances prevented them from providing their own voices to the soundtrack, so they were substituted by John Clive (John), Geoffrey Hughes (Paul), Pete Batten (George) and Paul Angelis (Ringo). The character of the Nowhere Man, Jeremy (voiced by Dick Emery), was, allegedly, based on Jonathan Miller.

Although it wasn't an enormous hit on release, *Yellow Submarine* has become a much-loved classic and was a huge seller when released on DVD in 1999. 'I like the Blue Meanies,' George noted. 'And the Apple bonkers. They never say anything, they just go along bonking people. That's a good idea, the more bonking the better.'

It's crying out for a sequel, frankly. *Yellow Submarine II: Back to Pepperland* anyone?

Let It Be (1970)

A voyeuristic look at the process of a group breaking up, *Let It Be* began with great intentions – the Beatles rehearsing and then performing an LP's worth of new material. But the rehearsals, at Twickenham in January 1969, were a disaster – Ringo was bored, Paul had his bossy head on, John was strung-out on smack and distracted by Yoko's presence, and George got so pissed off with the whole deal that he walked out.

Eventually, he agreed to finish the movie and the location was switched to Apple's basement studios and, ultimately, the roof of Savile Row for a live performance.

Michael Lindsay-Hogg's editing decisions often seem to highlight the tensions within the band; some of those present have suggested that the atmosphere wasn't nearly as bad as *Let It Be* makes out (that certainly wasn't a view shared by either John or George, though).

Still, if its only contribution to the Beatles archive was the exhilarating version of 'Get Back' as the police arrive to break up the rooftop concert, *Let It Be* is a worthwhile document of a painful month.

WE ALL WANNA CHANGE THE WORLD
– The Beatles' LPs

The Magical Mystery Tour (1967)

Initially released in the UK as a six-song double EP, in America the addition of all the non-album singles of 1967 – 'Strawberry Fields Forever', 'Penny Lane', 'All You Need Is Love', 'Baby You're A Rich Man' and 'Hello Goodbye' – gave Capitol an LP for the Christmas market. Although it wasn't released in Britain until 1976, *The Magical Mystery Tour* is now regarded as a vital part of the Beatles CD discography – the missing link between *Sgt. Pepper's* and *The Beatles*.

It was recorded between 25 April and 7 November 1967. During these (somewhat confusing and, indeed, confused) six months, 'All Together Now' and 'It's All Too Much' from the *Yellow Submarine* soundtrack, the B-side 'You Know My Name (Look Up The Number)' and several unnamed (and apparently tedious) jam sessions were also taped.

As this period coincided with a lot of herbal being smoked, the death of Brian Epstein, a sojourn in Greece where they almost bought an island, meeting the Maharishi, George going to San Francisco and finding it full of 'horrible spotty drop-out kids on drugs' and the – gloriously haphazard – filming of *The Magical Mystery Tour* film itself, it's astonishing that the Beatles managed to record *anything* of much interest.

The soundtrack songs are a strange bunch. 'I Am The Walrus' is, of course, a masterpiece. 'The Fool On The Hill' and the title song are also terrific. But 'Blue Jay Way' is a genuine contender for the worst thing the Beatles ever recorded, an overproduced melange of production tricks without anything resembling a tune to go with it.

DON'T PASS ME BY
The famous Ringo Starr

There's a joke, which some have attributed to John Lennon. It admits that Ringo Starr was not the best drummer in the world; in fact, goes the punch line, he wasn't even the best drummer in the *Beatles*.

It's a rather cruel – and inaccurate – assessment and, frankly, doesn't sound like the kind of thing that John would say at all. (In fact, this author can clearly recall it being told by British comedian Jasper Carrott in the early 80s.)

Indeed, when asked about Ringo, John (as with Paul and George) were always keen to stress that their drummer had been playing with one of Liverpool's best bands before the Beatles were even a group. They'd known him for years, had played with him occasionally and poached him from the Hurricanes precisely because he was *good*.

Personality-wise, quite apart from his musical ability, Ringo was the perfect choice for the Beatles. He had the same sense of humour as the others. When they started making films it was Ringo who proved to be the most natural physical comedian and his performances in *A Hard Day's Night* and *Help!* would lead to a short, but interesting, acting career.

He was also, often, the one who could inject a note of earthy realism to the highfalutin, vainglorious schemes of his colleagues.

As a drummer, he certainly wasn't a virtuoso like his friend Keith Moon. But then, in the Beatles, he didn't need to be. His work was often understated but – as with Charlie Watts in the Stones – Ringo was the glue that held his band together.

Yet there are key performances – 'Ticket To Ride', 'Rain', 'She Said She Said', 'Strawberry Fields Forever', 'A Day In The Life', 'Long Long Long' – where he produced hugely influential drum-patterns that help to *make* the songs. It's no wonder he had blisters on his fingers after the way he played on 'Helter Skelter'.

Do You Want to Know a Secret?

Ringo loved his time in the Beatles – the bits that he can still remember, anyway – as evidenced by his joyous recollections in the *Anthology* series.

At heart, it's Ringo's show. Some of the most memorable moments of the project are his gleeful, down-to-earth memories; himself and George ('two shit-kickers from the 'pool') living it up in London, a friend of his mother's prediction – in 1958 – that he would one day be on *Sunday Night at the London Palladium*, or the point when he realised his life was changing (when, during a family visit, he was suddenly treated like minor royalty).

When the Beatles ended, people worried about how Ringo would fare in the harsh realities of a solo career, but they needn't have. Ringo's always been a born survivor (two major childhood illnesses that would have killed someone with less mental toughness are evidence of that).

Aided by his three former bandmates, he had a few hits in the early 70s, made some films (he's great in Claude Whatham's *That'll Be the Day*), married actress Barbara Bach, voiced *Thomas the Tank Engine* and now lives a jet-set lifestyle in California and Monte Carlo. Though he's had a few problems with health and the booze over the years, he remains one of the most popular men on the planet.

'We were honest with each other and we were honest about the music,' he once noted. 'The music was positive. The basic Beatles message was love.'

ACROSS THE UNIVERSE
Important radio performances

It's difficult from a modern perspective to understand how important BBC radio was to musicians in the early 1960s. In an era where the BBC held an absolute monopoly of the airwaves, getting a record played on a programme like *Saturday Club* – with an audience in tens of millions – could instantly transform someone's career.

Because of restrictions placed on the corporation by the powerful musicians' union, the BBC had a commitment to recording sessions by musicians in their own studios instead of simply playing their records (a situation that still – thankfully – exists to this day in parts of the BBC). Thus, when the Beatles got a session for the BBC Light Programme they would often perform not just their latest single, but other songs – often ones they never got around to recording properly at EMI.

Between 1962 and 1965, the Beatles recorded 52 shows for the BBC and, during the course of them, performed some 36 songs that never showed up on any of their records (35 were cover versions, just one was a Lennon/McCartney original, 'I'll Be On My Way', which they gave to Billy J Kramer).

Inevitably, audience recordings exist of virtually all the Beatles' radio appearances and in the 1970s bootlegs emerged featuring some of these performances (notably, the *Yellow Matter Custard* LP). Finally, in the 1980s, the BBC woke up to the potential in their own vaults but were then horrified to discover that they'd junked most of the original tapes.

After a lengthy search, private recordings of most of the shows were discovered and the BBC did a series of *The Beatles At The Beeb* programmes culminating, in 1994, in the release of a double-CD package under the same name.

Here are some of the radio shows that the Beatles graced:

Teenager's Turn – Here We Go (8 March 1962)

The Beatles passed their audition for BBC Radio in Manchester on 12 February, producer Peter Philbeam noting that they were an unusual group 'more C&W with a tendency to play music', although he was less sure about Paul McCartney as a vocalist.

The band were booked for their first radio show, which was recorded at the Playhouse Theatre, Manchester, where they shared the bill with the Northern Dance Orchestra directed by Bernard Herrmann. The Beatles performed 'Dream Baby', 'Memphis, Tennessee' and 'Please, Mr Postman'.

Saturday Club (26 January 1963)

The renowned *Saturday Club* – presented by Brian Matthew and produced by Bernie Andrews – was the most influential and popular of the BBC Light Programme's pop shows. The Beatles would make a dozen appearances on *Saturday Club* after this first session on which they performed 'Some Other Guy', 'Love Me Do', 'Please Please Me', 'Keep Your Hands Off My Baby' and 'Beautiful Dreamer'.

Pop Goes the Beatles (4 June 1963)

So popular were the Beatles becoming by the summer of 1963 that they got their own radio show. Four *Pop Goes the Beatles* editions were initially recorded – this was the first, at the Aeolian Hall Studio in Bond Street – featuring compere Lee Peters. As the *New Musical Express* noted, 'the Beatles will sing five or six numbers in each presentation. R&B material will be strongly featured.'

Each show started with a manic beat-adaptation of 'Pop Goes The Weasel' (according to legend the Beatles had problems recording it and had to be helped by their guests on the first show, the Lorne Gibson Trio). The main performance of interest here is a rip-roaring version of 'The Hippy Hippy Shake' with Paul on vocals. The listening audience of this show was 2.8 million.

Easy Beat (23 June 1963)

Recorded on 19 June, live in front of a very enthusiastic audience at the Playhouse Theatre in London, the Beatles storm through a four-song set ('Some Other Guy', 'Thank You Girl', 'A Taste Of Honey', 'From Me To You').

Pop Goes the Beatles (16 July 1963)

The success of the first *Pop Goes the Beatles* shows encouraged the BBC to commission eleven more, starting with this one, recorded at their Maida Vale Studios on 2 July. There was a new compere, Rodney Burke.

This is one of *the* great Beatles performances – in addition to their own 'There's A Place' they recorded Elvis's 'That's All Right (Mama)', Chuck Berry's 'Carol', a stunning version of Arthur Alexander's 'Soldier Of Love (Lay Down Your Arms)', Carl Perkins' 'Lend Me Your Comb' and the Jodimars' 'Clarabella'. ('Three Cool Cats' and 'Sweet Little Sixteen' were also recorded but not broadcast.)

From Us to You (26 December 1963)

The first of an irregular series of Bank Holiday specials recorded for the BBC (on 18 December at Paris Studio in Regent Street). The Beatles performed a selection of their recent hits and, also, a mildly amusing version of 'Tie Me Kangaroo Down' with Rolf Harris. Other guests included Kenny Lynch and Joe Brown and the Bruvvers.

From Us to You (30 March 1964)

Recorded at the BBC's Piccadilly Studios in late February, this show was compered by Alan Freeman and included some witty repartee ('George, is it true that you're a connoisseur of the classics?' 'No, it's just a rumour!') and eight songs.

Top Gear (16 July 1964)

The first episode of a new late-evening show put together by the *Saturday Club* team. The Beatles performed live-in-the-studio versions of 'Long Tall Sally', 'Things We Said Today', 'A Hard Day's Night', 'And I Love Her', 'I Should Have Known Better', 'If I Fell' and 'You Can't Do That'.

The Beatles (Invite You to Take a Ticket to Ride) (7 June 1965)

The Beatles' final BBC special – with compere Denny Piercy – included versions of 'Everybody's Trying To Be My Baby', 'I'm A Loser', 'The Night Before', 'Honey Don't', 'Dizzy Miss Lizzy', 'She's A Woman' and 'Ticket To Ride'.

Do You Want to Know a Secret?

Where It's At (25 November 1967)

By this time, the Light Programme had become Radio 1. This show, hosted by Kenny Everett and Chris Denning, featured the world premiere of the *Magical Mystery Tour* EP (and the only time the BBC would play 'I Am The Walrus', subsequently banned for the dreadful crime of containing the word 'knickers', for several years) together with a lengthy interview with John. Also featured was a short McCartney solo performance of a song usually described as 'All Together On The Wireless Machine', which has appeared on many Beatles bootlegs.

TIME FOR TEA AND *MEET THE WIFE*
Important television performances

Classic products of the television age, the Beatles were among the first musical phenomena whose rise was propelled by, not just radio and newspaper exposure, but also the visual medium of TV. Dates refer to the initial broadcast.

Thank Your Lucky Stars (19 January 1963)
The Beatles' first appearance on the Sunday ABC variety show on which they were to become a virtual house-band over the next eighteen months. Introduced by host Brian Matthew, they mimed to 'Please Please Me' and, across the country, screaming at TV sets became a new national sport for teenage girls.

Ready Steady Go (4 October 1963)
Broadcast live from North London, *RSG* – slogan: 'The Weekend Starts Here!' – was in many ways the embodiment of sixties pop-TV. The Beatles appeared four times and this was their debut, being interviewed by Keith Fordyce and guest-host Dusty Springfield (Cathy McGowan was on holiday that week) and miming to 'Twist And Shout', 'I'll Get You' and 'She Loves You'.

The Mersey Sound (9 October 1963)
Don Haworth's extraordinary documentary of the Beatles' first few months of stardom was filmed over four days in late August. It includes incredibly serious interview material (miles removed from the frivolous questions they were usually asked by journalists), concert footage and staged promo clips for 'Love Me Do', 'She Loves You' and 'Twist And Shout' that are still used by EMI to this day. Much of the material is familiar through *Anthology*, but see the original in its entirety if you can, it's a pocket gem.

Drop In (3 November 1963)
The Beatles' trip to Sweden in October was a triumph, with some well-received concerts and this fantastic TV performance. Live in the studio, with an audience

of enthusiastic fans sitting just inches from them, the Beatles seem to be really enjoying themselves as they power through 'She Loves You', 'Twist And Shout', 'I Saw Her Standing There' and 'Long Tall Sally' then join in clapping along to the show's theme tune.

Local Scene Extra (25 November 1963)

The Beatles' TV appearances with comedians usually went well and this Granada show in which they were interviewed with Ken Dodd (on 'tattyfilarious' form) is no exception. Particularly amusing is Doddy asking the Beatles for ideas for an 'earthy name' so he can form his own beat group. 'Sod,' suggests George!

Afterwards, on an imaginative set with a *Daily Echo* backdrop and an enlarged 'Beatex' camera, the Beatles mimed 'I Want To Hold Your Hand' and 'This Boy' (although the latter wasn't broadcast until a subsequent edition).

Juke Box Jury (7 December 1963)

It is hard to overemphasise just how important a show *Juke Box Jury* was. Presented by the suave David Jacobs, the reaction of the panel to a record could, literally, make or break it in chart terms. On this special edition, the Beatles were the panel – voting 'Hit' or 'Miss' to discs by the Swinging Blue Jeans, Elvis Presley and Billy Fury among others.

The Ed Sullivan Show (9 February 1964)

In front of an estimated audience of 70 million, America discovered 'these youngsters from Liverpool'. As George would later note, 'even the criminals took an hour off'. The Beatles performed 'All My Loving', 'Till There Was You', 'She Loves You', 'I Saw Her Standing There' and 'I Want To Hold Your Hand'. Historic stuff.

The Morecambe and Wise Show (18 April 1964)

'It's the Kaye Sisters!' Eric and Ernie *and* the Beatles? Talk about TV heaven. This performance was actually filmed in December the previous year (hence the Beatles choice of songs, 'This Boy', 'All My Loving' and 'I Want To Hold Your Hand'). The highlight is a (scripted) comedy routine in which George and, particularly, John get some cracking one-liners, followed by Ernie performing the standard 'Moonlight Bay' with the band.

Around the Beatles (6 May 1964)

Fitted in around the filming of *A Hard Day's Night*, this Jack Good-produced Rediffusion TV special featured the Beatles performing a (rather laboured) spoof of Shakespeare's *A Midsummer Night's Dream* and a terrific (if mimed) musical section. This featured 'Twist And Shout', 'Roll Over Beethoven', 'I Wanna Be Your Man', 'Long Tall Sally', 'Can't Buy Me Love', a 'hits medley' of 'Love Me Do', 'Please Please Me', 'From Me To You', 'She Loves You' and 'I Want To Hold Your Hand', and a spectacular cover of the Isley Brothers' 'Shout'.

The Beatles in Nederland (8 June 1964)

With Ringo in hospital with tonsillitis, John, Paul, George and Jimmy Nichol travelled to Holland for two shows in Amsterdam and this remarkable TV appearance. The band are interviewed by Berend Boudewijn, which is amusing enough, but it's nothing compared to what happens when they perform a mimed selection of their hits.

By the time they get to 'Long Tall Sally' and 'She Loves You', some of the audience begin dancing with the group. In 'Can't Buy Me Love', you can hardly see Beatles for dancing Dutchmen as Mal, Neil and Derek Taylor fight their way through the crowd to get John, Paul and George (who seem to think this is hilarious) off stage. Meanwhile, poor Jimmy is left on his drum-riser playing away to the backing tracks. It has to be seen to be believed.

Top of the Pops/Doctor Who (15 April/22 May 1965)

The Beatles usually filmed clips for their latest single (and, sometimes, the B-side, too) for *Top of the Pops*; this one is particularly interesting because, although the original tape of this performance of 'Ticket To Ride' has long since been junked, 25 seconds of it was subsequently used in the *Doctor Who* episode 'The Executioners'. It's worth watching, if only to see Ian Chesterton (William Russell) dancing like a physics teacher crushing cockroaches at a sixth-form disco.

Blackpool Night Out (1 August 1965)

The band appeared on several editions of *Big Night Out* (hosted by the terminally unfunny Mike and Bernie Winters). This one is the most widely seen, featuring live performances of 'I Feel Fine', 'I'm Down', 'Act Naturally', 'Ticket To Ride', 'Yesterday' ('and now, for Paul McCartney of Liverpool, opportunity knocks!') and 'Help!'

Top of the Pops (16 June 1966)

The Beatles' only live appearance on the BBC's flagship music show. They performed 'Paperback Writer' and 'Rain', introduced by a hyperventilating Pete Murray.

Not Only … But Also (26 December 1966)

John's friendship with Dudley Moore and Peter Cook stretched back to 1964 when he appeared on the first episode of *Not Only … But Also*, reading poems from *In His Own Write*. For this legendary episode (in which Cook and Moore performed a song called 'The LS Bumble Bee' that, for years afterwards, turned up on Beatles bootlegs purporting to be a *Sgt. Pepper's* out-take) John was, again, invited to appear.

During a lengthy sequence, Cook plays an American TV presenter – Hiram J Pipesucker – investigating 'Swinging London'. He arrives at the entrance to the AdLav nightclub (actually, a public lavatory in Boardwick Street) to be met by a doorman (John) who refuses him entry until bribed. Comedy genius.

Our World (25 June 1967)

Here's a good idea – let's preview our new single on a live TV show going out, by satellite, to 150 million people. Mass-marketing via global communication is born as the Beatles, effectively, create the concept for MTV, Live Aid, etc.

A part-mimed performance of 'All You Need Is Love' in Abbey Road, with an audience of friends (Jagger and Richards, Keith Moon, Eric Clapton, Mike McCartney, etc.). Introduced by Steve Race, George Martin said 'play' and they did. And the world listened.

WE ALL WANNA CHANGE THE WORLD
– The Beatles' LPs

The Beatles (The White Album) (1968)

Coming back from India with more songs than they knew what to do with, the Beatles hit upon a smart idea for the first LP on their Apple label. Make it a double and include *everything*. So, from 30 May to 17 October 1968, they virtually lived in the studio. And Yoko Ono lived with them.

Geoff Emerick – their engineer since *Revolver* – quit because the atmosphere got so bad. George Martin was frequently bored and sometimes left sessions in the hands of Chris Thomas. A depressed Ringo departed for a fortnight and the band carried on without him (Paul plays drums on 'Back In The USSR' and 'Dear Prudence'). A deeply pissed-off George managed four songs on the LP but tried over a hundred takes to get a fifth – 'Not Guilty' – to work, felt it still wasn't right and buggered off to Greece.

Yet amid all this the Beatles, almost despite themselves, were creating a masterpiece. A massively flawed, hugely self-indulgent and bitterly personal masterpiece, admittedly. One that includes 'Rocky Raccoon'. And 'Wild Honey Pie'. I mentioned flawed, right?

But, really, that's all incidental. Where *The Beatles* is good, it's brilliant and where it's bad, it's still *fascinating*. This is the Beatles LP that you'd take to a desert island because of the variety and the strangeness of the moods it creates – alternatively bright and yet also often sinister and shadowy. What Miles calls the LP's 'sprawling chaos'.

Thirty-four songs were recorded, thirty made the record ('Not Guilty' and 'What's The New Mary Jane?' missed out, while 'Hey Jude'/'Revolution' became the biggest-selling Beatles single). Many of them could have done with some further group input but, by this stage, they were acting virtually as each other's session-men, if that. This fact was evidenced by Paul recording 'Why Don't We Do It In The Road' (a song John admired greatly) without asking for John's help.

The session that produced 'I Will' (a *really* simple song) went on all night although, even here, the Beatles could throw off a little gem like the medley of McCartney's 'Step Inside Love' and the make-it-up-as-we-go-along 'Los Paranoias' between takes.

What we are left with is a luck-dip into a Pandora's box of delights: 'Dear Prudence', 'While My Guitar Gently Weeps', 'Happiness Is A Warm Gun', 'I'm So Tired', 'Blackbird', 'I Will', 'Julia', 'Sexy Sadie', 'Helter Skelter', 'Long Long Long' and, yes, 'Revolution 9'. It's a strange, baffling trip. It's challenging. It's sometimes unnerving. But it's often – far more than you may have been led to believe – wonderful.

Would it have been better as a single LP as George Martin wanted? Who cares; it wasn't. History will judge what we got. This author is with McCartney all the way on that score. 'It was *the bloody Beatles White Album.* Shut up!'

YOU MAY SEE THE MEANING OF WITHIN
Further inspirations for Beatles songs

- In a 2004 interview with *Guitarist*, Paul McCartney noted the influence of JS Bach's 'Bouree in E Minor' on 'Blackbird'.

- John wrote 'Please Please Me' in the style of Roy Orbison's 'Only The Lonely'. The lyrics were, in part, inspired by a linguistic pun in Bing Crosby's 'Please' (1934).

- Another early Lennon song, 'Do You Want To Know A Secret?' had its genesis in memories of his mother singing 'I'm Wishing' from Disney's *Cinderella* when John was a child.

- 'I'll Be Back', as Lennon admitted, was based on the descending guitar line of Del Shannon's 1961 hit 'Runaway'.

- The lyrics of 'The Inner Light' were adapted by George from Lao-Tse's *Tao Te Ching*, which had been recommended to him by Cambridge scholar Juan Mascaró following George's appearance on *The Frost Programme* in October 1967.

- According to both Paul and George, Stockhausen's 1955 electronic composition *Gesang der Jünglinge* was a major inspiration to the sound of 'Tomorrow Never Knows'.

- George Martin's skeletal, wintry arrangement for 'Eleanor Rigby' was inspired by Bernard Herrmann's score for François Truffaut's *Fahrenheit 451*.

- The repetitive guitar lick on 'I Feel Fine' was, seemingly, a homage to a similar riff heard in Bobby Parker's 1961 single 'Watch Your Step'.

- Many commentators suggest the influence of the Beach Boys' *Pet Sounds* – notably 'God Only Knows' – on 'Here, There And Everywhere', though the dates never quite seemed to fit (Paul's ballad was recorded in June 1966, while *Pet Sounds* wasn't released until July). However, Beach Boy Bruce

Johnston *was* in London in May, armed with acetates of the LP, and he met John and Paul (along with Keith Moon) at his suite in the Aldwych Waldorf. A few days later, sitting by John's swimming pool in Weybridge and waiting for his partner to get out of bed, Paul wrote the song.

○ John's harmonica solo on 'Love Me Do' was inspired by the playing of Delbert McClinton on Bruce Channel's 'Hey Baby'. The Beatles appeared on the same bill as Channel and McClinton at the Tower Ballroom in New Brighton in June 1962.

○ 'Polythene Pam' was, according to John, 'remembering a little event with a woman in Jersey and England's answer to Allen Ginsberg'. This was beat-poet Royston Ellis, whom the Silver Beetles had backed at the Jacaranda Club in 1960. The date of this apparent three-in-a-bed romp was 8 August 1963, it actually took place in Guernsey and the woman involved was Ellis's then-girlfriend, Stephanie.

○ Written in the style of Fats Domino, the piano opening to 'Lady Madonna' is an instantly recognisable lift from Johnny Parker's playing on Humphrey Littleton's 1956 single 'Bad Penny Blues'.

○ 'It's All Too Much' featured lyrics borrowed from the Merseys' 'Sorrow'. The trumpet solo directly quotes *Prince of Denmark's March* by Jeremiah Clarke (1674–1707).

○ One the most important Beatles songs, 'Happiness Is A Warm Gun', was partly written in India in April 1968 as a series of overtly sexual metaphors concerning Yoko Ono (see the version on *Anthology 3*). It was completed some months later when John and Derek Taylor made up a series of lyrics from random images while tripping on acid. The title was allegedly inspired by the cover of a gun magazine that George Martin brought into Abbey Road. (No one has yet provided a convincing explanation as to why dear old George would have such a publication.)

All the Beatles were excited by the song and its complex structure and switches of time signature. It subsequently took on greater significance for Paul as the Beatles completed recording it on 25 September 1968, the night that his future wife Linda flew into London at Paul's invitation.

I NEED A FIX COS I'M GOING DOWN
Self-confessed drug references

The Beatles were clearly no strangers to stimulants. They were introduced to Benzedrine even before they left Liverpool. Then came amphetamines in Hamburg, marijuana in New York in 1964 and LSD in London a year later (spiked by George's naughty dentist).

Paul had a flirtation with cocaine during the *Sgt. Pepper's* sessions and John and Yoko spent a long dark winter of the soul during 1968–69 in the grip of heroin addiction.

Many people – usually those with specific political agendas – suspected that some of the Beatles' best-known songs were *full* of allusions to drugs. Several *were* written under the influence ('She Said She Said', 'I Am The Walrus', for instance). But that's slightly different from saying they're *about* drugs. Subsequently, all four Beatles were quite open about their usage of 'herbal jazz cigarettes' and various other substances.

So, ignoring all speculation on things like the initials in 'Lucy In The Sky With Diamonds' (almost certainly *not* a drug reference), here are a number of lyrics that are. And there's surprisingly few. (Note, all specific Beatle-denials have been taken at face value, hence the absence of both 'Happiness Is A Warm Gun' and 'Fixing A Hole'.)

'She's A Woman'
The Beatles' first reference to pot-smoking in the line 'turn me on when I get lonely'.

'Day Tripper'
'*That* was a drug song,' noted John in 1970. 'I liked the word.'

'Got To Get You Into My Life'
'It describes [Paul's] experience taking acid. I think that's what it's about,' Lennon told *Playboy*. 'It's actually about pot,' McCartney corrected some years later.

Do You Want to Know a Secret?

'With A Little Help From My Friends'
Note the line about getting high. 'It was the pot era, we had to slip in a little reference,' Paul later confessed.

'A Day In The Life'
Specific to the 'turn you on' lyrics. As Paul later wrote: 'John and I gave each other a knowing look: "Uh-huh, it's a drug song."'

'Get Back'
For those who think California grass is something you sit on …

I'VE GOT NO TIME FOR TRIVIALITIES
Twenty bits of Beatles-trivia that defy categorisation

1. Dick Rowe, the Decca A&R chief, infamously rejected the Beatles after their audition for the company in January 1962. 'Groups with guitars are on their way out,' he reportedly told Brian Epstein.

Eighteen months later, Mr Rowe was the laughing stock of the music industry. He did, however, somewhat redeem his reputation when, on George Harrison's recommendation, he signed the Rolling Stones in May 1963.

2. One of several ideas for a proposed third Beatles movie was a script written by the controversial playwright Joe Orton. The writer met Brian Epstein and Paul McCartney for dinner on 24 January 1967 and entertainingly wrote about their conversation in his diary. Paul had enjoyed Orton's current play *Loot* saying, 'The only thing I [usually] get from the theatre is a sore arse.'

Orton produced a brilliant – if completely unfilmable – script entitled *Up Against It*, in which the Beatles would have played transvestite anarchist guerrillas. It was rejected, in April, by Epstein. 'An amateur and a fool,' wrote Orton. 'He isn't equipped to judge the quality.'

Four months later, Orton was dead, murdered by his lover Kenneth Halliwell, who then took his own life. 'A Day In The Life' was played at Orton's funeral.

3. Another idea that the Beatles toyed with around this time was doing a film with Patrick McGoohan, the maverick Irish actor/producer whose TV show, *The Prisoner*, was a cult hit during 1967. Sadly, nothing came of the collaboration. Also under consideration at one time or another were Richard Condon's novel *A Talent for Loving* and a mysterious script called *Shades of a Personality* in which the Beatles would have played four different facets of the same character.

4. John Lennon's first book of prose and poetry, *In His Own Write*, was published in 1964 and quickly became a bestseller. Lennon had been writing this kind of acerbic nonsense since he was at school and had previously published examples of it in his 'Beatcomber' column in *MerseyBeat*.

Do You Want to Know a Secret?

To promote the book, John appeared on the BBC's prestigious *Tonight* programme in March 1964, interviewed by Kenneth Allsop. It was a question from the journalist as to why John didn't produce songs that employed the clever wordplay of *In His Own Write* and his second book *A Spaniard in the Works* that led John to compose what he considered to be his first 'serious' lyric, 'In My Life'.

Several high-profile reviews of *In His Own Write* suggested the influence of authors as diverse as James Joyce, Edward Lear and Lewis Carroll. While freely admitting his admiration for Carroll, Lennon claimed not to have read the others (in an interview with *World of Books* in June 1965, he also rejected a suggestion that he made a deliberate use of onomatopoeia, claiming he didn't even know what the word meant). In fact, John's main inspirations were likely to have been *The Goon Show* and the eccentric comedian Stanley Unwin.

Not everyone was impressed. Uxbridge MP Charles Curran – a regular Lennon critic – used a speech in the House of Commons to pass haughty and dismissive comment of the book's 'pathetic state of sub-literacy', adding that Lennon seemed 'to have picked up bits of Tennyson, Browning and Robert Louis Stevenson while listening with one ear to the football results on the wireless'.

5. The Beatles' instantly identifiable collarless jackets and silver-grey mohair suits were made by their outfitter Dougie Millings, the 'Tailor to the Stars', who had a shop on Old Compton Street, Soho. Dougie made a brief appearance in *A Hard Day's Night* as the tailor who has his tape measure cut by John.

6. One of the Beatles' more surprising – but certainly sincere – friendships was with the singer Alma Cogan. They first met when they both appeared on *Sunday Night at the London Palladium* in 1964 and discovered that they had a shared sense of humour.

Alma lived with her mother and sister in an apartment off Kensington High Street and this became a regular hang-out for the Beatles prior to Alma's untimely death in 1966. Alma's dinner parties introduced the band to the more establishment end of show business (Lionel Blair, Bruce Forsyth, Tommy Steele and Frankie Vaughan were among those they met, and the band's friendship with songwriter Lionel Bart can also be traced back to Stafford Court).

One of the first people Paul visited after writing 'Yesterday' (which he was initially convinced was someone else's song) was Alma to ask if she recognised it.

7. Some of the most instantly recognisable images of the Beatles come from a single day – 28 July 1968 – which has become known as 'The Mad Day Out'.

The Beatles, accompanied by celebrated photojournalist Don McCullin and Tom Murray of the *Sunday Times*, used a series of London locations like Hyde Park, St Katherine's Dock, St Pancras Church Park, Old Street Station and the garden of Paul's place in St John's Wood. Many of the photos were subsequently used on the poster given away with *The White Album*.

8. The earliest known film of the Beatles is a 30-second super-8mm colour clip, without sound, of John, Paul, George and Pete Best playing at what appears to be a Valentine's Day dance. Two five-second fragments of the film were broadcast on *ITN News* on 15 May 1996.

It is alleged to be from 14 February 1961, which would mean that it was filmed at either the Cassanova Club or Litherland Town Hall. However, doubt has been cast on that date as the band were wearing their leather stage clothes, which they didn't acquire until April 1961 when they returned to Hamburg for their second residency.

It seems, therefore, that the film must come from a year later, but that also creates a problem as the Beatles only known performance on 14 February 1962 was at the Cavern and it's *certain* that the film wasn't shot there.

9. On 9 February 1967 as Paul prepared to travel to the studio (the Beatles were recording 'Fixing A Hole') a dishevelled individual turned up at his door claiming to be Jesus. Paul invited the man along to the session on condition that he sat quietly in the corner while the Beatles were working. Which he did. After the session finished, Jesus thanked Paul for his company and left. Paul never saw Jesus again.

10. The cherry-red Gibson SG that George Harrison played throughout the *Revolver* sessions was sold for £294,000 at Christie's in New York in December 2004. George had given the guitar away, in 1969, to Pete Ham of Badfinger.

11. Another group that the Beatles were friendly with were the Monkees – despite press attempts to drum up controversy about the American group's alleged lack of musical ability and their TV show's debt to *A Hard Day's Night* and *Help!*

During February 1967, Mickey Dolenz and Mike Nesmith were invited to the orchestra session for 'A Day In The Life'. They also attended a party at McCartney's house, an event Dolenz would immortalise in his song 'Alternate Title'.

12. One of the Beatles' big stage-numbers in Hamburg was Ray Charles's R&B standard 'What'd I Say'. With its repetitive riff and call-and-response vocals that encouraged audience participation, it's reported that the band often played versions that lasted up to half an hour. Another much-requested song they played live but never got around to recording was Paul singing James Ray's waltz-time 'If You Gotta Make A Fool Of Somebody'.

13. The much-admired guitar solo on 'Nowhere Man' was played by Harrison on a Sonic Blue Fender Strat – one of a pair that he and Lennon bought during the *Help!* sessions. McCartney has said that the exceedingly treble-y guitar sound on the record was achieved by persuading Norman Smith to put the guitars through several layers of faders. 'We were always forcing them into things they didn't want to do,' Paul noted.

14. In the summer of 1966, *New Musical Express* journalist Alan Smith interviewed each of the Beatles on the subject of their dreams. While a few of the revelations probably say more about what they were smoking at the time than anything psychological, a few fascinating nuggets emerged.

McCartney displayed classic anxiety symptoms when revealing that he dreamed of plane crashes and being caught naked in the street. Crashing planes also featured prominently in Harrison's dreams. Lennon described an out-of-body experience and a recurring dream of being surrounded by money but being unable to carry as much as he wanted to.

15. Most of the major figures in Apple – before Allen Klein became involved in the company – were either trusted Beatle-employees (Neil Aspinall, Derek Taylor), part of their social circle (Peter Asher, Miles, Terry Doran) or members of NEMS with whom they'd worked for years (Alistair Taylor, Peter Brown, Tony Bramwell).

One of the most important players in the company was the notorious Alexis Mardas. With the benefit of hindsight, John would recall in 1972, 'I brought in Magic Alex and [things] just went from bad to worse!'

Working as a TV repairman when John first met him, Mardas was a Greek engineer who headed Apple Electronics and devised various outrageous conceits that appealed to John's sense of the absurd. Lennon considered him a genius. Unfortunately, as George would subsequently point out, 'He didn't *do* anything. When we finally got him to make a recording studio, we walked in and it was chaos.'

16. In 1964, when virtually anything Beatles-related was being sold to the eager American public, the Santa Monica-based Vee-Jay Records, the company who owned the rights to most of the Beatles' 1963 recordings, also released *Hear The Beatles Tell All*.

Recorded in August 1964, the LP – edited and scored by Lou Adler – intercut 'live in-person interviews' conducted by Jim Steck and Dave Hull over a percussion track by noted session man Hal Blaine.

A mixture of press-conference inanity and some interesting revelations (the Lennon interview, in the wake of the Hollywood Bowl show, which takes up the entire first side is particularly good), the LP remains one of the most sought-after examples of Beatlemania product despite having been reissued in 1982 by Charley Records.

17. Some of the most treasured Beatles-items are the records they issued to fan-club members each Christmas from 1963. It was Tony Barrow who originally devised the idea, chiefly to avoiding someone having to individually reply to letters from an estimated 80,000 members.

The first two discs were scripted by Barrow (although it was evident, by 1964, that the Beatles enjoyed sending up his rather corny style – note John's statement that he'll be writing another book soon 'it says here'). The 1965 disc is particularly interesting as it includes some pointed social comments on Vietnam amid the mock-Scouse hilarity. In 1966, McCartney devised a pantomime – *Everywhere It's Christmas* – in the style of his home recordings of the era. The next year, the experimental *Christmas Time (Is Here Again)* took a pop at various radio and television clichés.

The final two discs were pieced together by Kenny Everett from tapes he made with the Beatles individually. The 1968 record was great, featuring some inspired Lennon-lunacy (the story of two balloons called 'Jock and Yono'), a lovely McCartney acoustic ballad ('He's come all the way from Stokely Carmichaels-on-Sea') and George, in America, introducing Tiny Tim singing 'Nowhere Man'. However, the 1969 record was pretty much a John-and-Yoko solo vehicle on which Paul, George and Ringo appear for approximately fifty seconds in total.

18. On 16 February 1964, while in Miami for their second *Ed Sullivan Show* appearance, a photo opportunity was arranged for the Beatles to meet Cassius Clay, then in training for his forthcoming heavyweight championship fight with Sonny Liston. Reportedly, when the future Muhammad Ali told the Beatles that they weren't as dumb as they looked, Lennon replied, 'No, but *you* are.'

19. New Year's Eve 1966, and George Harrison is refused entry to the swanky Annabel's nightclub for that most 1950s of crimes, 'not wearing a tie'. George, Patti, Brian Epstein and Eric Clapton instead celebrate the New Year at the Lyon's Corner House restaurant near Piccadilly Circus.

20. The Beatles remain, 35 years after they split, the artists with the most Christmas number one singles – four – in the UK.

WE ALL WANNA CHANGE THE WORLD
– The Beatles' LPs

Yellow Submarine (1969)

The soundtrack to the animated *Yellow Submarine* movie was, for many years, regarded as an embarrassing blot on the Beatles' discography. Six songs (including the title track and 'All You Need Is Love', both of which every self-respecting fan had already) and a second side containing George Martin's (admittedly rather lovely) orchestral score.

Of the four 'new' songs, the *Sgt. Pepper's* cast-off 'Only A Northern Song' was miserably lightweight. 'All Together Now' and 'It's All Too Much' from sessions in May and June 1967 were better, the latter in particular being one of George's most interesting pieces. 'Hey Bulldog' (recorded in February 1968 along with 'Lady Madonna', 'The Inner Light' and 'Across The Universe') was a belter – although it didn't fit into the film very well.

The worst-selling 'official' Beatles LP ever, finally, in 1999 with the release of the movie on DVD, Apple decided to remedy matters. They released *The Yellow Submarine Songtrack* on CD, which added nine further songs from the movie to the six on the original LP ('Eleanor Rigby', 'Love You To', 'Lucy In The Sky With Diamonds', 'Think For Yourself', 'Sgt. Pepper's Lonely Hearts Club Band', 'With A Little Help From My Friends', 'Baby You're A Rich Man', 'When I'm Sixty-Four' and 'Nowhere Man').

Given a gentle (but highly effective) remix polish, the songs – especially 'It's All Too Much' – had never sounded better. All of sudden, *Yellow Submarine* became an essential purchase. Especially if Blue Meanies have been sighted in your area.

ARRIVE WITHOUT TRAVELLING
Places mentioned in Beatles songs

Georgia
One of the 13 original states of the US, admitted to the union in 1788. Mentioned in 'Rock And Roll Music'.

Penny Lane
Both a street and a district in Liverpool 18, once described by jazz musician George Melly as a 'dull suburban shopping centre' far removed from the hallucinogenic wonderland described in 'Penny Lane'. The barber's shop (Bioletti's), the bank and the fire station were all there, however.

Strawberry Field
A Victorian Salvation Army orphanage in Beaconsfield Road, Woolton, a short distance from John's family home. Immortalised in 'Strawberry Fields Forever'.

Bishopsgate
A busy thoroughfare that runs north through the City of London past Liverpool Street Station. Mentioned in 'Being For The Benefit Of Mr Kite'.

The Isle of Wight
Made up of a pleasant collection of holiday resorts in the Solent off Portsmouth, Hampshire. John and Paul travelled there (probably in April 1963) to visit Paul's cousin Betty Robbins and her husband Mike, who ran a bar in Ryde. There is some speculation that this would subsequently inspire 'Ticket To Ride'. Certainly the Isle is mentioned in 'When I'm Sixty-Four'.

Blackburn
A rather unbeautiful mill town in Lancashire – population c.140,000. 'A Day In The Life' alleges there are many holes there.

The Albert Hall

Large circular concert venue in South Kensington built around 1870. The Beatles played there on a couple of occasions in 1963, and it is mentioned in 'A Day In The Life'.

The Eiffel Tower

This 985-feet-high monument on the Champ-de-Mars in Paris was erected in 1889 and, until 1930, remained the highest construction in the world. It was designed by, and named after, Gustave Eiffel (1832–1923). Climbed by semolina pilchards in 'I Am The Walrus'.

Los Angeles

Massive garish-if-occasionally-surprising metropolis in California. The Beatles stayed there several times during the 60s and Ringo now lives there. Mentioned in 'Blue Jay Way'.

Miami Beach

Resort in Florida where the Beatles had a holiday in February 1964. Where they flew into on 'Back In The USSR'.

Moscow, Ukraine and Georgia

The capital city of, and two regions that in 1968 formed part of, the Soviet Union. Moscow is now in Russia and the Ukraine and Georgia gained their independence in 1991. All namechecked in 'Back In The USSR'.

The Black Hills, South Dakota

Mining area in the north of the United States. South Dakota was admitted to the union in 1889. Alluded to in 'Rocky Raccoon'.

Hollywood

Suburb of Los Angeles and, for many years, the centre of the US film and entertainment industry. Mentioned in 'Honey Pie'.

Kirkcaldy

Royal borough in Fife, Scotland. Population 47,000. Named in 'Cry Baby Cry'.

Do You Want to Know a Secret?

Southampton, Gibraltar, Paris, Amsterdam, Vienna and London

The Lennons' European tour of March and April 1969 immortalised in 'The Ballad Of John And Yoko'.

Tucson and California

City in southern Arizona and a state on the west coast of the United States, both mentioned in 'Get Back'.

Lime Street

Popular Liverpool thoroughfare, mentioned in 'Maggie Mae'.

EXPERT TEXTPERT
Hilariously over-the-top critique concerning the Beatles

- 'In twenty years time, nothing of them will survive.' – F Newton in *New Statesman* (November 1963)

- 'The Mersey Sound is the voice of 80,000 crumbling houses and 30,000 people on the dole.' – *Daily Worker* (December 1963)

- 'Harmonic interest is typical of their quicker songs too and one gets the impression they think simultaneously of harmony and melody, so firmly are the major tonic sevenths and ninths built into their tunes, and the flat-sub-mediant key-switches, so natural is the Aeoline cadence at the end of "Not A Second Time" (the chord progression which ends Mahler's "Song of the Earth").' – William Mann in *The Times* (December 1963) in an article which also described chains of padiatonic clusters in 'This Boy'.

- 'I've met them. Delightful lads. Absolutely no talent.' – Noel Coward (1964)

- '75 per cent publicity, 20 per cent haircut and 5 per cent lilting lament.' – *New York Herald Tribune* (February 1964)

- 'The Beatles are a passing phase; symptoms of the uncertainty and confusion of the times.' – Billy Graham (1964)

- 'There is something magical and sinister about repetitive siblings. The Beatles inspire terror, awe and reverence. I had no idea they looked so similar – just marginal differences on an identical theme. And with that hair, they remind me of the Midwich Cuckoos.' – Jonathan Miller (1964)

- 'The Beatles' MBE reeks of mawkish, bizarre effrontery to our wartime endeavours.' – Richard Pape, returning his own award, and quoted in the *Daily Mirror* (1965)

- 'I would like to congratulate Joe Meek on his letter regarding the Beatles. He is so right in drawing attention to the amount of pleasure this group gives to people of all ages … As a medical practitioner I welcome anything which contributes to human happiness.' – Letter to the *New Musical Express* (August 1966)

⊙ 'The Beatles are musically trash; long-haired slobs who screech and thump in a mixture of unrelated noise that would insult the ear of any self-respecting orang-utan. When the revolution is ripe, the Communists will put the Beatles on television in order to hypnotise US youth.' – Reverend David A Noebel of the Christian Crusade, quoted in *Newsweek* (August 1966)

⊙ 'A decisive moment in the history of Western civilisation.' – Kenneth Tynan reviewing *Sgt. Pepper's Lonely Hearts Club Band* in *The Times* (May 1967)

⊙ 'What's happened to the Beatles? They rose as heroes of a social revolution. They were everybody's next-door neighbours, the boys whom everybody could identify. Now, four years later, they have isolated themselves. They have become contemplative, secretive, exclusive and excluded.' – *Daily Mail* (June 1967)

⊙ 'Neither Lennon nor McCartney were world-beaters in school, nor have they had technical training in music. For them to have written some of their songs is like someone who had not had physics or math inventing the A-bomb … Because of its technical excellence it is possible that this music is put together by behavioural scientists in some "think tank".' – Dr Joseph Crow of the John Birch Society (July 1967)

⊙ 'I declare that the Beatles are Divine Messiahs. The wisest, holiest, most effective avatars the human race has yet produced, prototypes of a new race of laughing freemen.' – Dr Timothy Leary (1968)

⊙ 'I wish to express my disgust at the latest Beatles' single which, in my mind and in any other true pop lover's [sic] is, or should be, nominated the worst record of 1968.' – Geoffrey Henderson (Benfleet) in a letter to the *New Musical Express* concerning 'Hey Jude' (August 1968)

⊙ 'If you think that pop music is mind-blowing noise, then the Beatles have done it better – on distant shores of the imagination that others have not even sighted.' – Tony Palmer reviewing *The Beatles* in the *Observer* (November 1968)

⊙ 'It's a catchy tune, but until it was pointed out to me, I never realised that the "friends" were assorted drugs with such nicknames as "Mary Jane",

"Speed" and "Benny".' – US Vice-President Spiro T Agnew on 'With A Little Help From My Friends' (1970)

- 'Three bars of "A Day In The Life" still sustain me, rejuvenate me, inflame my senses and sensibilities.' – Leonard Bernstein (1977)

- 'There's not one good lyric, if you compare them with the likes of Ray Davies or a career like Dylan's. The best they got was awful Lennon philosophising and adolescent whinging. They did nothing but arselick their entire career.' – Luke Haines in *Uncut* (2001)

NOT A SECOND TIME
Beatles songs that refer to other Beatles songs

Apart from obvious repetitive vernacular clichés (the references to 'diamond rings' in 'Can't Buy Me Love', 'I Feel Fine' and 'If You've Got Troubles', for instance), the Beatles developed an interestingly self-mythologising habit of mentioning their own previous lyrics. It was something that Lennon seemed especially fond of.

- 'All You Need Is Love' refers to 'She Loves You'.

- 'I Am The Walrus' refers to 'Lucy In The Sky With Diamonds'.

- 'Lady Madonna' refers to 'I Am The Walrus'

- 'Glass Onion' refers to 'Strawberry Fields Forever', 'I Am The Walrus', 'Lady Madonna', 'Fixing A Hole' and 'The Fool On The Hill'.

- 'Savoy Truffle' refers to 'Ob-La-Di, Ob-La-Da'.

- 'Come Together' refers to 'I Am The Walrus'.

- 'Carry That Weight' refers to 'You Never Give Me Your Money'.

WE ALL WANNA CHANGE THE WORLD
– The Beatles' LPs

Abbey Road (1969)

Recorded after *Let It Be* (the record, the movie *and* the court case) but released first, the Beatles' final studio LP is a curious affair. It *sounds* magnificent, easily their best recorded set of songs (they were finally on eight-track after years of having to perform miracles of tape manipulation). Conversely, it *feels* slightly hollow.

Recorded between 22 February and 20 August 1969, Lennon was hardly present (through a combination of circumstances, including a car crash). He stuck around long enough to give the band 'Come Together', 'Because', 'I Want You (She's So Heavy)' and a couple of fragments for the McCartney-conceived long medley on side two. Then, within days of the LP's completion, he told his colleagues that he was leaving for good.

In John's absence, *Abbey Road* was dominated, for the only time in the Beatles' career, by McCartney and Harrison working closely to create a lush-sounding work. Harrison brought in his recently acquired Moog synthesizer and the sound is all over the LP. He also wrote two bona fide standards, 'Something' and 'Here Comes The Sun'.

Macca's main contributions were the perceptive 'You Never Give Me Your Money' and the Beatles' final gasp of greatness 'Golden Slumbers'/'Carry That Weight'/'The End'. Ringo had a good moment, too, with 'Octopus's Garden'.

Essentially *Abbey Road* is a clearing of the decks before the final dissolution of the band. 'An LP like they used to make,' George Martin noted. It wasn't, quite, but it was close enough for everyone to, albeit briefly, believe that the Beatles could survive into the 1970s as a going concern.

YELLOW SUBMARINE
The appearance of various Beatles in *The Simpsons*

Many issues continued to divide the Beatles into the 1990s, but one thing that united Paul, George and Ringo was guest appearances on *The Simpsons*.

Ringo Starr in 'Brush With Greatness'
(11 November 1991)

Seeking inspiration for her recently reactivated artistic career (her latest project is to immortalise Monty Burns on canvas), Marge is delighted to receive a reply from Merrie Old England to a letter she wrote in 1966.

Ringo, it seems, is currently living in a castle with his butler, Weatherby, and still answering 25-year-old fan mail. His favourite colour is blue and he is partial to tea and crumpets. In reply to Marge's queries, he confirms we have French fries in England (but we call them chips) and thinks her portrait of him is so 'gear' that he hung it on the wall.

George Harrison in 'Homer's Barbershop Quartet'
(30 September 1993)

The simple story of the B-Sharps' (Homer, Apu, Seymour and Barney) rise from obscurity in Moe's Cavern to stardom and their bitter break-up. All of this may sound suspiciously familiar (the sacking of Chief Wiggum, an LP called *Bigger Than Jesus*, Barney's Japanese conceptual-artist girlfriend, the rooftop finale) but that was probably a coincidence.

George meets Homer at the Emmy awards and directs him to the biggest pile of brownies Homer has ever seen. Subsequently, George watches the B-Sharps reforming to sing 'Baby's On Board' on Moe's roof before noting, dismissively, 'Nah, it's been done!'

Paul and Linda McCartney in 'Lisa the Vegetarian' (15 October 1995)

When Lisa decides to become a vegetarian she seeks the spiritual counsel of the world's two most noted herbivores, Paul and Linda.

The couple often spend time in Apu's garden in the shade (Apu having been, apparently, 'the fifth Bee-atle' since their Maharishi phase). Paul also reveals that 'Maybe I'm Amazed' contains a backward message (but it's just a vegetarian recipe). And that he isn't dead.

Technically, all four Beatles have appeared in *The Simpsons*. In 'Last Exit to Springfield' (11 November 1993), Lisa's dream sequence at the dentists' turns into a missing scene from *Yellow Submarine* ('Look, it's Lisa in the sky'; 'No diamonds though'), until the ship crashes into a campy cartoon of Queen Victoria ('Lord, 'elp us!').

SPEAKING WORDS OF WISDOM
Quotes (part 3)

⊙ John on meeting dignitaries: 'They were always threatening to make bad publicity if we didn't meet their daughter with braces on their teeth. It was always the police chief's daughter or the Lord Mayor's daughter, the most obnoxious kids, because they had the most obnoxious parents.'

⊙ Paul, interviewed for *So Far Out, It's Straight Down*, on the subject of Swinging London: 'I wish the people that look in anger at the weirdoes, the happenings, the psychedelic freak-out, would instead look with nothing, with no feeling, be unbiased about it.'

⊙ John, on receiving a Variety Club Award from the future Prime Minister Harold Wilson: 'Thanks for the purple heart, Harold.'

⊙ George, when asked for his feelings on the Vietnam war: 'The words "Thou shalt not kill" mean that. Not "Amend, Section A".'

⊙ Paul, asked about the psychologists, journalists and social thinkers who try to analyse the Beatles' success: 'I don't think they know what they're talking about.'

⊙ Ringo, on the generation gap: 'We're just as against the things our parents stood for as they are in America, but we don't hate our parents for it.'

⊙ John, on the accusation that the Beatles had been snubbing Liverpool: 'The people that are moaning about us not being here are people that never even came to see us when we were here. We could count on our fingers the original fans we had.'

⊙ George, on how he liked being described as the Prime Minister's secret weapon: 'I didn't get the bit where they said, "Earning all these dollars for Britain." Are we sharing it out or something?'

⦿ John: "'How long are you gonna last?' You can be big-headed and say, "We're gonna last ten years." But as soon as you've said that you think, "We're lucky if we last three months.'"

DAY TRIPPER
What the Beatles were doing on important days in history

It's often alleged that if you can remember the 1960s then you weren't really there. The Beatles bestrode the decade like a colossus. For many who *were* there, the band and their music were the only important things that happened between 1962 and 1970.

However, it's probably worth noting that some other stuff *did* occur that didn't involve the Beatles directly. Here's a selection of such events, together with details of exactly what the Beatles were up to at the time.

10 July 1962
On the day that the Telstar satellite brought the birth of the global communication age with the first televised cross-Atlantic link-up, the Beatles were playing a lunchtime session at the Cavern.

22 October 1962
As humanity lurched towards a possible third World War with the beginning of the Cuban missile crisis, and Kennedy and Khrushchev sought ways to avoid mutually assured destruction, at least the punters at Queen's Hall, Widnes had something to celebrate. They got to see the Beatles.

24 November 1962
One of history's most influential TV shows, *That Was The Week That Was*, began flaying the establishment with its satirical barbs on this particular Saturday night in London. Meanwhile, the Beatles may have caught part of the show backstage after they'd finished their set at the Lido Ballroom in Prestatyn.

14 February 1963
Future Prime Minister (and sometimes professional Beatles fan) Harold Wilson became the leader of the Labour Party, following the death of Hugh Gaitskell.

One of Wilson's constituents, John Lennon, and his colleagues were playing a Valentine's Day dance at the Locarno Ballroom in Liverpool.

3 March 1963
The spy Kim Philby defected to Russia at (more or less) the very moment that the Beatles played their final date on the Helen Shapiro Tour at the Gaumont Cinema in Hanley. Were these two events connected? Perhaps we'll never know.

5 June 1963
While John Profumo, the War Secretary, was making his dramatic resignation speech to the House of Commons, having been caught lying concerning his relationship with Christine Keeler, the Beatles were on stage at the Odeon Cinema, Leeds as part of the Roy Orbison Tour.

8 August 1963
At the very moment when Buster, Ronnie and their mates were pulling off the Great Train Robbery and blagging over two million quid, the Beatles had a cast-iron alibi. They were performing at the Candie Gardens Auditorium in Guernsey. How convenient.

28 August 1963
It's doubtful whether the audience at the Odeon Cinema, Southport, made as much noise during the Beatles' set as the hundreds of thousands in Washington who were witnessing Martin Luther King's 'I have a dream' speech.

26 October 1963
As Sir Alec Douglas-Home announced his first cabinet after succeeding Harold Macmillan as Prime Minister, the Beatles had little time to reflect on their mysterious absence from a portfolio. They were playing two shows at Kungliga Tennishallen in Stockholm. Meanwhile, in Newcastle upon Tyne, this author was being born – which was quite important to him if not, necessarily, anyone else.

22 November 1963
As the world gave a collective gasp of horror at the unfolding events in Dallas, and the murder of John Kennedy, the Beatles went on stage at the Globe

Cinema, Stockton-on-Tees. The tragic day had begun so well, with the release of *With The Beatles*.

23 November 1963

The BBC began their flagship SF-show, *Doctor Who*. The Beatles may have seen 'An Unearthly Child', the opening episode, before their gig at the City Hall, Newcastle.

28 March 1964

In the Solent, the pirate station Radio Caroline, which was to have such an effect on the listening habits of Britain's youth, began broadcasting. The Beatles, meanwhile, were taking a break from filming *A Hard Day's Night* – John, Cynthia, George and Patti were in Ireland, Ringo was spending the Easter weekend at Woburn Abbey, while Paul remained in London.

14 June 1964

In South Africa, ANC leader Nelson Mandela was jailed for life for political offences. It would be 26 years before he was released, eventually to become his country's president. The Beatles, or at least three of them plus temporary drummer Jimmy Nichol, were in Melbourne and would be joined later in the day by a jet-lagged Ringo who, after recovering from tonsillitis, had just arrived in Australia.

2 August 1964

In the early hours of the morning, the North Vietnamese navy attacked the US destroyer the *Maddox* in the Gulf of Tonkin – an incident which escalated the inevitable slide towards war in Southeast Asia. Meanwhile, the Beatles were topping the bill at the Gaumont, Bournemouth.

15 October 1964

In one of history's most remarkable 24 hours, Soviet Premier Nikita Khrushchev was deposed, in Britain Labour won the general election thus ending thirteen years of Conservative rule, while China became the world's third nuclear power with their first atomic test. Yet again, while something important was happening elsewhere, the Beatles were stuck in 'happening' Stockton-on-Tees, playing the

Globe Theatre and being interviewed by Tyne Tees television for *North East Newsview*.

21 February 1965
Black nationalist Malcolm X was assassinated in New York. In London, the Beatles were actually having a day off, packing, prior to flying to the Bahamas to begin filming *Help!*

14 August 1965
The most violent outbreak of racial tension in the US, the Watts riots, were finally contained by the National Guard in Los Angeles after having raged out of control for three days. Half a continent away, the Beatles were in CBS Studio 50 in New York taping a six-song performance for *The Ed Sullivan Show*.

7 October 1965
In London, the Post Office Tower, three years in construction, finally opened. With John and Paul busy writing songs for the forthcoming *Rubber Soul* sessions, today's major news story was a report suggesting that Pete Best was to sue Ringo over comments the latter made in an interview with *Playboy*.

11 November 1965
Rhodesian President Ian Smith made his long-threatened declaration of independence from Britain. The Beatles were in Abbey Road, putting the final touches to 'Wait' and 'I'm Looking Through You' and recording 'You Won't See Me' and 'Girl'. By the early hours of the next day, they had finished *Rubber Soul*.

5 May 1966
Ian Brady and Myra Hindley were jailed for life for the Moors Murders. On a less dreadful note, the Beatles spent most of the day perfecting George's backward guitar solo for 'I'm Only Sleeping'.

30 July 1966
The greatest day in the history of the world. 'Some people are on the pitch, they think it's all over ...' The Beatles probably watched the match, as they were back in London after their disastrous Philippines tour. However, in the US, a storm

was brewing as the teen-magazine *Datebook* had published John's 'Jesus' interview the day before. Even as various radio DJs in the southern states prepared themselves with a mass burning of Beatles merchandise, *Yesterday And Today* hit No. I in the Billboard charts.

13 August 1966

This day saw the beginning of the cultural revolution in Mao's China, with a state-orientated attack on 'revisionism' and an ideological purging of counter-revolutionary tendencies. The Beatles were bringing their own revolution to Detroit, playing two sets at the Olympic Stadium.

4 January 1967

Donald Campbell, attempting to be the first man to break 300 mph on water, died when his *Bluebird* turbo-jet crashed on Coniston Water. The Beatles, meanwhile, were in Abbey Road working on 'Penny Lane'.

20 March 1967

The tanker *Torrey Canyon* was wrecked in storms off the Cornish coast, leading to the worst environmental disaster in Britain to that date. The Beatles, knee-deep in the *Sgt. Pepper's* sessions, spent the day recording the vocals for 'She's Leaving Home'.

29 April 1967

Ten thousand people crammed into the Alexandra Palace for the *14 Hour Technicolour Dream*, a benefit party for the underground *International Times* newspaper, described as 'the first tribal gathering of the British beautiful people'. For once, the Beatles were actually involved, John and George both attending. A tripping Lennon apparently watched Yoko Ono perform.

5 June 1967

The Six-Day War between Israeli and Arab forces began. The Beatles were inactive today – in the case of Paul and George, perhaps because they were hung over after attending, the evening before, the famous Jimi Hendrix Experience concert at the Saville Theatre at which Jimi opened his set with 'Sgt. Pepper's Lonely Hearts Club Band'.

9 October 1967

Revolutionary spirit and left-wing hero Che Guevara was killed in Bolivia by government forces. Within a couple of years every self-respecting student would have a copy of Alberto Korda's art-print of Che decorating their bedroom wall. John Lennon, himself no stranger to the bedroom wall of students was, coincidentally, celebrating his 27th birthday.

31 January 1968

The Tet offensive began as communist forces launched a series of attacks on South Vietnam. Meanwhile, George was completing work on his first solo project, the *Wonderwall* soundtrack, at Abbey Road.

17 March 1968

One day after the My Lai massacre in Vietnam, Britain's more politically active students assembled at the US embassy in Grosvenor Square, London. The subsequent clashes with the police seemed to symbolise the schism between the forces of order and the new freedoms of the younger generation. Or, alternatively, it was just a good punch-up on a Saturday night with the lads. John, George and Paul were still at the Maharishi's retreat in India, although Ringo was back in London, having described Rishikesh as 'just like Butlins'.

2 May 1968

In Paris, French students took protest one stage further, rioting in the streets and attempting to bring down De Gaulle's government. The Beatles, having returned from India, were taking a break prior to the announcement of the formation of Apple the following week.

5 June 1968

US presidential candidate Robert Kennedy was assassinated in Los Angeles in a year in which political murder became sadly commonplace. In London, the Beatles were in Abbey Road recording Ringo's 'Don't Pass Me By'.

21 August 1968

The invasion of Czechoslovakia by Warsaw Pact forces, threatened since Alexander Dubcek began his liberalisation policies in the spring, finally happened. The Beatles would respond to this in an odd way, recording 'Back In The USSR' just 24 hours later. Meanwhile, today was spent working on 'Sexy Sadie'.

6 October 1968

'The troubles' began in earnest with Republican riots in Londonderry against sectarian discrimination. The Beatles spent the early hours of the morning in Trident Studios recording 'Savoy Truffle'.

16 January 1969

Czech student Jan Palach attempted suicide in Prague's Wenceslas Square by setting fire to himself in protest against his country's occupation by the Soviet Union. He died five days later, a national hero. Having stopped the *Get Back* rehearsals at Twickenham due to George's temporary departure, the rest of the Beatles spent the day making plans to switch locations to Apple's new basement studio. Work would recommence a week later.

21 July 1969

As Neil Armstrong and Buzz Aldrin left Apollo 11 and made their giant leaps for mankind, and Edward Kennedy appeared in court over his 'leaving the scene of an accident' at Chappaquiddick the day before, the Beatles were in Abbey Road recording 'Come Together'.

9 August 1969

In Bel Air, Charles Manson's Family cult murdered actress Sharon Tate and four friends in a frenzied attack that, in some twisted way, they claimed had been 'inspired' by the Beatles' 'Helter Skelter'. In London, the Beatles were taking the weekend off, having shot the cover photo for *Abbey Road* on Friday afternoon.

13 April 1970

As the world reacted to Paul's announcement, three days earlier, that the Beatles were effectively no more, they were given something else to be concerned about when Apollo 13 had their 'problem' and NASA frantically tried to bring their astronauts home.

WE ALL WANNA CHANGE THE WORLD
– The Beatles' LPs

Let It Be (1970)

Recorded – during what Lennon described as 'a miserable month in hell' – in January 1969, *Let It Be*, for all its good intentions ('the Beatles as nature intended') was a disaster from start to finish. Infighting broke out during the Twickenham rehearsals before they had recorded a note. The songs were a pretty substandard lot, nobody could be bothered half the time, and when they could it usually led to more arguments.

Out of the sessions, at Apple, and the live performance on the roof of Savile Row on 30 January, came just about enough halfway-decent recordings to fill an LP. 'I've Got A Feeling' had a bit of soul, 'For You Blue' some nice slide guitar, and McCartney's trio of standards, 'Two Of Us', 'Let It Be' and 'The Long And Winding Road' were always going to impress the fans. And they got a great single out of it, too, 'Get Back'/'Don't Let Me Down' (the latter, mysteriously, left off the eventual LP). Billy Preston's presence helped and, on occasions, it even sounds as though the band actually had a bit of fun.

However, the project lay in the can for over a year (Paul, George and Ringo returned to the studio in January 1970 to record 'I, Me, Mine', the final Beatles recording) and, as 1969 turned into 1970, John listened to the tapes, decided they were unreleaseable, and – without asking McCartney – called in Phil Spector to do something that the sessions were supposed to be a rejection of: 'production'.

Whether you regard what Spector did to 'The Long And Winding Road' as sacrilege (McCartney certainly did) or as the only thing possible to cover John's incompetent bass playing, the fact is that *Let It Be* emerged, was pretty much disliked by everyone, but still sold millions.

Finally, in 2003, Paul got his wish for the un-Spectored tapes to be released. *Let It Be … Naked* stripped out the between-song chatter and the two fragments 'Maggie Mae' and 'Dig It', reinstated 'Don't Let Me Down' and sounded … pretty good, actually. A bonus disc containing some fascinating snippets from the Twickenham tapes (including the amusing 'Fancy My Chances With You') was also included.

There are those of us, however, who still hanker to have the full twelve-minute version of 'Dig It' (26 January recording) finally released in all its ragged, amateurish glory.

MOLLY LETS THE CHILDREN LEND A HAND
Musically fab offspring

Zak Starkey
Followed in his dad's drumbeats with an impressive career as a member of the Who, Johnny Marr's Healers and, latterly, Oasis.

Julian Lennon
Sold a lot of records in the 80s. His biggest hit was 'Too Late For Goodbyes' on which he sounded uncannily like his dad.

Dhani Harrison
The spitting image of George, it seems that guitar ability also runs in the genes. Played on George's 2000 remake of 'My Sweet Lord' and his final LP, *Brainwashed*.

James McCartney
Macca Junior appears on his father's *Flaming Pie* and *Driving Rain*.

Sean Lennon
Has had a spasmodically interesting career, including some work with his mother, and with the band Cibo Matto.

THE END
The break-up of the Beatles

On 10 April 1970, Paul McCartney announced that he had left the Beatles. Ironically, he was the last member to do so. Ringo had, briefly, quit during 1968, George a year later and, in September 1969, John told his colleagues that he was leaving.

What followed was a bitter and nasty divorce. In June, Lee Eastman wrote to Allen Klein asking that the Beatles' partnership be dissolved. George Harrison's reply to Paul was, 'You'll stay on the f*cking label. Hare Krishna.'

In November, Paul filed a lawsuit against John, George, Ringo and Apple Corps. 'I agonised over suing my best mates,' he noted. The case reached the High Court on 31 December. A writ sought 'a declaration that the partnership and business carried on by the plaintiff and the defendants under the name of The Beatles & Co., and constituted by a deed of partnership dated 19 April 1967 made between the parties hereto, ought to be dissolved.'

The case opened on 19 January 1971 with Justice Stamp presiding. David Hurst, Paul's QC, argued that among the reasons for bringing the case were that the Beatles had long since ceased to perform together and that McCartney had never been given audited accounts in the four years since the partnership was formed. On 18 February, further grievances were added, specifically that Klein's company, ABKCO, had altered 'The Long And Winding Road' without consulting Paul.

'Artistic disagreements arose, particularly between Paul McCartney and John Lennon, who [wrote] most of the songs,' claimed Hurst. 'In January 1969, Mr Klein was introduced by John Lennon, who proposed that he be appointed manager. George Harrison and Ringo Starr were also keen. McCartney did not trust Klein and wanted a New York law firm, Eastman & Eastman, where his father-in-law and brother-in-law were partners.'

Morris Finer QC, representing the defendants, suggested that Klein had 'saved the Beatles from almost total bankruptcy'. John's affidavit stated that 'the

Beatles' company, Apple, was full of hustlers and spongers'. George talked extensively about 'the only serious row between Paul and me' (the one in January 1969 seen in *Let It Be*) while Ringo was 'shocked and dismayed' by the whole affair.

Klein vigorously defended himself: 'McCartney never accepted me as his manager, but the partnership did. McCartney has accepted all the benefits which I have negotiated. As regard to my ability to make deals, I am content to be judged on my record.'

On 26 February, Paul became the only Beatle to give personal evidence. He said that the Beatles had stopped working as a group and suggested that it was clear from recent recordings by John and George that neither saw themselves as Beatles. On his recent album (*John Lennon/Plastic Ono Band*), John had listed things he didn't believe in, one of which *was* Beatles.

It was also disclosed that, under the terms of his management contract, Klein was only entitled to 20% of any improvements he negotiated on existing contracts. However, when Capitol raised the Beatles royalty rate from 17.5% to 25%, Paul's accountants discovered that Klein had paid himself 20% of the entire amount — half a million pounds over what he'd been due. 'That was the only thing we caught him on,' said Paul. 'We couldn't send him to jail, but at least we could get a judgement.'

On 12 March, the judge found in favour of Paul and appointed James Spooner as receiver for all the Beatles' business interests. John, George and Ringo left court with an abrupt 'No comment'. (It's been alleged that they then drove to Paul's home in Cavendish Avenue where John put a couple of bricks through the window. This has never been confirmed.)

Throughout 1971, Paul and John vented their fury at each other through their music ('Too Many People', and 'How Do You Sleep?', for instance). In November, the real nastiness started when Paul was interviewed by *Melody Maker* and said 'I just want the four of us to get together somewhere and sign a piece of paper saying it's all over. But John won't do it.' Lennon replied, venomously, two weeks later with a letter published in the same magazine which bordered on libellous.

During December the two met in New York in an attempt to patch up their relationship. This seems to have been mostly successful and, for the rest of Lennon's life, he and Paul remained on reasonable, if occasionally bitchy terms.

They met infrequently (and jammed together only once, in LA in 1974), but they talked on the phone every few months and at least stopped calling each other names in public.

In March, 1973, Klein's management contract with John, George and Ringo expired and wasn't renewed. When asked why, John admitted, 'Let's just say that, possibly, Paul's suspicions were right.'

On 19 December 1974, Paul and George were both in New York with a view to signing a document ending the Beatles' partnership (Ringo had already signed, in England). They were initially thwarted as John's astrologer told him the time wasn't right. John finally signed the document eight days later at Disneyworld, which he was visiting with Julian.

The Beatles & Co. partnership was formally dissolved on 9 April 1975, almost five years to the day since Paul first announced the split, in a private hearing attended by none of the Beatles. A sad and somewhat anticlimactic end to arguably the greatest musical partnership of all time.

PAPERBACK WRITER
A Beatles bibliography

Hunter Davies's official 1968 biography, *The Beatles*, despite Lennon's subsequent low opinion of it ('a whitewash'), is still the most intimate of Beatles studies. After all, there aren't many people who can claim to have been in the same room as John and Paul when they composed 'With A Little Help From My Friends' or in Abbey Road when John had his acid trip when recording 'Getting Better'.

The other generally well-regarded biography is Philip Norman's *Shout!* (1981), although Norman's retrospective portrayals of Lennon and McCartney can seem obscenely sycophantic concerning the former and depressingly hostile towards the latter.

Harrison and McCartney both participated in official biographies that are worth seeking out: the former with Derek Taylor – *I, Me, Mine* (1981) – the latter, Barry Miles's *Many Years From Now* (1997). Both contain many fascinating revelations (and Harrison's is full of the guitarist's trademark pithy wisdom). However, both are also, in places, as much about what they *don't* say as what they do.

The same could be argued concerning the band's occasionally enlightening, self-written *The Beatles Anthology* (2000) and also Lennon's two extraordinary soul-bearing interviews with *Rolling Stone* (*Lennon Remembers*, Jann Wenner, 1973) and *Playboy* (*The Playboy Interviews*, David Sheff and G Barry Golson, 1981). These, at different times in John's life, give startling insights into both the best and the worst of Lennon's complex character.

John's friend Pete Shotton (with Nicholas Schaffner) wrote an affectionate and readable account of their relationship (*John Lennon in my Life*, 1984), while Cynthia Lennon's *A Twist of Lennon* (1978) also paints a picture of John as a flawed but, essentially, likeable and humane individual troubled by occasional inner demons.

Both are certainly decent alternatives to Albert Goldman's infamously salacious *The Lives of John Lennon* (1988) and to Ray Coleman's dry, uncritical *Lennon: The Definitive Biography* (1985).

Do You Want to Know a Secret?

Journalistic studies of the Beatles always fall short of the first written — American author Michael Braun's extraordinary 1964 life-on-the-road exposé, *Love Me Do: The Beatles Progress*.

Both Spencer Leigh's *Speaking Words of Wisdom* (1991) and Keith Badman's *The Beatles: Off the Record* (2000) are worthy attempts at producing a coherent narrative from this most non-linear of histories. Also recommended, in this regard, is Barry Miles's reliably complete *The Beatles Diary* (1998).

For an almost unbearably intimate look at the Beatles imploding in January 1969, see Doug Sulpy and Ray Schweighardt's *Get Back: The Unauthorized Chronicle of the Beatles' Let It Be Disaster* (1997).

George Martin's lovingly compiled deconstruction of the *Sgt. Pepper's* sessions (*Summer of Love*, 1994 with William Pearson) is worth the attention of fans, while Derek Taylor's *It Was Twenty Years Ago Today* (1987) provides another insider-view on the same era.

A less obvious aspect of the group's story can be found in Andy Babiuk's handsome *Beatles Gear* (1995) — a visually stunning study of the Beatles' instrumentation that, with double-page photos of Rickenbackers and Gretsches, borders on guitar pornography!

An often-neglected area of the Beatles' career, their recordings pre-EMI, is covered in superb detail in Hans Olof Gottfridsson's *From Cavern to Star Club* (1994).

For a critique on the band's musical output, there's really only one book — the late Ian MacDonald's revealing *Revolution in the Head* (1994). You may not agree with every opinion (MacDonald's assassination of 'Across The Universe' is particularly brutal) but you'll feel like an intellectual when you are reading it. The book's reception on either side of the Atlantic — wildly appreciated in Britain, somewhat coldly dismissed in America — says much about the perspectives of fans in different parts of the world.

That said, several authors before MacDonald had tackled the tricky subject of analysing the band's discography: William J Dowlding's *Beatlesongs* (1989), Roy Carr and Tony Tyler's lovably forthright *The Beatles: An Illustrated Record* (1974) and Wilfrid Mellers *Twilight of the Gods: The Beatles in Retrospect* (1973) were all praiseworthy efforts.

Finally, Mark Lewisohn's *The Beatles Live!* (1986), *The Complete Beatles Recording*

Sessions (1988) and *The Complete Beatles Chronicle* (1992) are the standard reference works by which all other books on the Beatles will be judged.

All factual information, dates and quotations in this book have been drawn from a variety of previously published sources. Besides those mentioned above, the following books were consulted during the preparation of this text:

Badman, Keith, *The Beatles After the Break-Up*, 1999.

Barrow, Tony, *Meet the Beatles*, 1963.

Burdon, Eric, with J Marshall Craig, *Don't Let Me Be Misunderstood*, 2001.

Clayson, Alan, *The Quiet One: A Life of George Harrison*, 1991.

Clayson, Alan and Leigh, Spencer, *The Walrus Was Ringo*, 2003.

Cott, Jonathan and Dalton, David, *The Beatles Get Back*, 1970.

DiLello, Richard, *The Longest Cocktail Party*, 1972.

Fletcher, Tony, *Dear Boy: The Life of Keith Moon*, 1998.

Friede, Goldie, Titone, Robert and Weiner, Sue, *The Beatles A to Z*, 1980.

Fulpen, HV, *The Beatles: An Illustrated Diary*, 1982.

Granados, Stefan, *Those Were the Days*, 2002.

Harry, Bill, *The Ultimate Beatles Encyclopedia*, 1992.

Howlett, Kevin, *The Beatles at the Beeb*, 1982.

Ingham, Chris, *The Rough Guide to the Beatles*, 2003.

Lahr, John [ed], *The Orton Diaries*, 1986.

McCabe, Peter and Schonfeld, Robert, *Apple to the Core*, 1972.

Miles, Barry *Beatles in their Own Words*, 1978.

Patterson, R Gary *The Great Beatles Death Clues*, 1996.

Peebles, Andy, *The Lennon Tapes*, 1981.

Reinhart, Charles, *You Can't Do That!*, 1981.

Riley, Tim, *Tell Me Why: A Beatles Commentary*, 1988.

Sellers, Robert, *Very Naughty Boys: The Amazing True Story of HandMade Films*, 2004.

Shaffner, Nicholas, *The Beatles Forever*, 1977.

Shepherd, Billy, *The True Story of the Beatles*, 1964.

Southall, Brian, *Abbey Road*, 1982.

Terry, Carol D, *Here There and Everywhere*, 1985.

Turner, Steve, *A Hard Day's Write*, 1994.

Wiener, Allen, *The Beatles: The Ultimate Recording Guide*, 1993.

Williams, Allan and Marshall, Bill, *The Man Who Gave Away the Beatles*, 1975.

Also, the following periodicals: *New Musical Express, Melody Maker, Mojo, Record Collector, Q, Uncut, Rolling Stone, The Times,* the *Evening Standard,* the *Guardian, The Beatles Book Monthly.*

THOSE WHO LOOM LARGE IN MY LEGEND

My thanks to: Ian Abrahams, Martin Day, Diana Dougherty, Clay Eichelberger, Tony and Jane Kenealy, Mick Snowden, Colin and Graeme Topping, and Deb Williams for their contributions and encouragement.

'I hope we passed the audition ...'